I Came
Not Alone

To Joe & May
Here is your trip to the
Southlands - Enjoy - It's been
a lot of fun for me

I Came
Not Alone

by Jim Tarbell

Illustrations by John Fadeff
Maps by Rebecca Lafore and John Fadeff

RIDGE TIMES PRESS
CASPAR, CALIFORNIA

© RIDGE TIMES PRESS 1994

CASPAR, CALIFORNIA 95420

ISBN 0-934203-07-5

Illustrations by John Fadeff
Maps by Rebecca Lafore and John Fadeff

Library of Congress Catalog Card Number: 94-67007

Printed at Black Bear Press
Caspar, California
Published May, 20, 1994
987654321

Contents

Grains of Life   1

Media Madness   8

Acción Cívica   16

Life in Rancho Nirvana   24

Connections of Wealth   30

First Coming   40

Twice Flattened   49

Greatest Show in the Jungle   56

Rock Spirits in the Automobile Graveyard   61

Process to Processed   70

Bananas   78

An American Presence   88

Pachijal   95

Legitimacy   106

Santiago   115

To Porvenir   124

Argentine Migration   131

Back to the Bowels of the Beast   139

Afterword   143

Acknowledgements

A project that lasts eighteen years piles up a long list of people who helped along the way. I thank them all including my brother Pete who gave me a place to write these stories twenty years ago, and wife Judy who read, edited and typed them originally and has found herself dealing with them once again. I thank Patsy Gallagher who did the first editing eighteen years ago and I thank my three kids, Beca, Shamli and Crescent for encouraging me to put them into print now.

This second time around I received valuable help, far beyond anything expected, from Lucie Marshall and Russell Bartley, who both put their expert minds into examining these stories and providing invaluable suggestions for ways to improve them. John Fadeff's drawings add a dimension to the stories which I could never have created and the maps that he and Beca Lafore collaborated on are a wonderful addition to these tales. We've used a custom typeface designed by Dorsey Alexander for the dropcaps at the beginning of each chapter and I thank Liz and Judy for their design ideas.The cooperation of all the people at Black Bear Press and Ridge Times Press made my writing and production of this book possible. Finally I thank all my friends who have encouraged me in this venture. It has been a lot of fun.

Illustrations & Maps

Quito and the Northwest of Pichincha Province   Frontpiece

You're just what we're looking for. Isn't that right Oswaldo?   19

In the back of Acción Cívica's brown Chevy pickup.   47

It was a big crash that went Kawhomp!   65

You can't understand them and they can't understand you.   83

Although I came solo, I came not alone.   97

Route Through the Southern Cone   114

Dedicated to all Americans. These are stories we should know.

A Short History of a Long Story

World conquest has been the dream of many cultures and long the bane of the rest of the world. From the Chinese dynasties through Hitler's Germany history is replete with overt military efforts to control the known environs. Half of a millennium ago a new form of conquest arose from the merchants of the renaissance era. Great trading companies with their attendant collusions between private capital and governmental might, dominated territories and trade routes.

Two hundred years ago with the birth of the United States, this trend took on a new twist, with the government leading the way into new territories and private capital coming afterward to reap the benefits. When President Thomas Jefferson sent Lewis and Clark into the wilds of the "unknown" west, commercial prospects were a top priority. John Jacob Astor was quick to pick up on the significance of this expedition and used Lewis and Clark's findings as the basis for a commercial empire that established the first American settlement on the West Coast and became the first private monopoly and commercial trust in the world.

Money and commerce became the darling of Western adventurers and with the inauguration of President Andrew Jackson the greed inherent in manifest destiny became a legitimized cultural policy. From government financing of the railroads through the Spanish-American War which gave the Sugar Trust access to fertile plantations and merchants a secure route to the Orient, the US government led the way for the expanding commercial power of private economic interests which were becoming increasingly centralized in monopolies and financial trusts.

Through two World Wars and the arduous Cold War the US government served the needs of private-sector economic leaders by stabilizing markets and guaranteeing access to cheap labor and raw materials throughout the world. With pride and heroism the Twentieth Century was made the American Century.

Three quarters of the way through this century, as I eluded one American involvement in South East Asia, I was sent to another as an American Peace Corps Volunteer in South America. In January 1973, I found myself high in the Ecuadorian Andes sixty miles east of the Pacific coast. Fourteen years earlier Fidel Castro's revolution in Cuba had captured the imagination of broad sections of the Latin American populace who were now pressing for reforms which threatened US corporate access to needed resources in Latin America. The US responded with a series of diplomatic initiatives, including the Peace Corps, to ameliorate discontent throughtout Latin America.

By the time I arrived in Ecuador a long-term US policy of forsaking diplomatic initiatives and replacing them with military might was taking hold. Over the next twenty years from Chile to Chiapas, hundreds of thousands of Latin Americans died resisting the imposition of foreign commercial and political interests.

For two and a half years I witnessed this conquest and the resistance to it throughout the mountains and jungles of Ecuador and the rest of South America. Having never reconciled the cultural and political differences inherent in this conflict, I felt compelled to write these stories when I returned to the United States in 1975. These are stories of the new world conquest; the coming of the New World Order.

Twenty years later, the future is now. With the end of the cold war and the dominance of the global marketplace signaled by the passage of NAFTA and the General Agreement on Trades and Tariffs, the world is in the hands of the international marketplace. This new conquest remains repugnant to the cultures and traditions of the rest of the world. I offer these stories as an insight into the continuing Third-World resistance to this domination, to UN "peace efforts" to "stabilize" independent countries. Humans require a modicum of survival that provides for their needs and gives them maximum control over their daily lives. This is not what global capitalism has to offer.

Quito and The Northwest of Pichincha Province

COLOMBIA

ECUADOR

PERU

PACIFIC OCEAN

Lago San Pablo

Mt. Cayambe, 5790

To Lago Agrio

Otavalo

Guayllabamba

QUITO

o Nono

Guayllabamba

Tandayapa

Mt. Pichincha
4794

Pacto

Río Guayllabamba

Pachijal

San Miguel
de los Bancos

P I C H I N C H A

Santo Domingo
de los Colorados

Km 116 Km 113

E Q U A T O R

Puerto
Quito

To
Esmeraldas

To
Guayaquil

S

Railroads
Major Highways
Roads
Paths
Unfinished Roads

Mls.
Kms.

0   3   6
0   5   10

prepared by R. Lafore and J. Fadeff '94

Grains of Life

J ANUARY 6, 1973, Quito, Ecuador — El Día de los Reyes, the Day of the Kings, the celebration of the coming of the wise men and there three of us sat, bewildered, in the middle of an ancient city. We had just arrived, and in an odd twentieth-century way our arrival marked the coming of kings of a different sort.

Wise men? Not yet, but the following years in Latin America brought wisdom and a reality into our lives which we could not foresee: some fortuitous, some tragic — so goes the legacy of Uncle Sam *en América Latina*.

I was a Portland boy, raised among the dwindling firs of the great Northwest, where sprawling fingers of suburbia slipped over the west hills into the farmlands of the valley beyond. I had earned an economics degree in DC while working for a Republican congressman when a not-yet-dead military draft and lingering Vietnam War set me at odds with the Selective Service System. I emerged with a conscientious objector classification and an obligation to do two years alternative service. My interest in the dynamic between the industrialized and non-industrialized worlds led me to the Peace Corps — and this bench I was sharing in downtown Quito. My hair was closely shorn and I wore a staid, button-down shirt and clean, tan pants.

Next to me sat Emil H. Peterson. Raised in Council Bluffs, Iowa, the youngest of eight, he was different from the day of his birth, always into adventure and intrigue. He fled Council Bluffs for high school in St. Paul, and then went on to university training as an archeologist in Seattle and Mexico. Now he was in Quito. He had left his farm roots long ago and though the Peace Corps brought him to Ecuador to be a farmer, there was little chance he was going to spend two years doing that. He was cool: his hair was long, but not long enough to touch his shoulders. Each strand flowed into a manicured position. "Sheesh Tarbell," he would mock me, "so what's wrong with brushing your hair." It was a time when hair was important in American culture and that fact did not escape him; neither did the loose beads that always gracefully hung around his neck. On this day he wore a skin-tight body shirt with a low neck, long sleeves and soft-textured, light-brown pants that splayed out at the ankles below which he wore ever-present sandals. His appropriately round eyeglasses and trimmed mustache gave his tight, five-foot-eight body a handsome sprinkling of academia and fun.

Beef Jurtleson, the third of our threesome, hadn't left the farm until he found himself sitting on this antique stone bench 9,000 feet in the Andes and twenty miles from the earth's equator. Six-four, with shocking blond hair, he was a block of a guy with no pretense of being anything but what he appeared. Product of a small Iowa town and graduate of the state high-er-education system, he was ready to investigate the strange scents beyond the screen door. It was doubtful he would ever go back — but then, neither would Emil.

The previous night we had flown out of the utlra-modern New Orleans airport and stopped over in Panama at dawn where electric contraptions snapped at swarming bugs. Then mid-day blossomed as we arrived high in the Andes where descendants of the Incas flow through lush rolling hills a mile and a half above the sea. Quito: one hundred and fifty years ago it was the seat of the Royal Spanish Audiencia and three hundred years before that it was the northern capital of the Inca Empire which had replaced the rule of another culture farther back in time.

In the late afternoon gray, Emil, Beef and I had stepped through the richly wooded lobby of our aging hotel into an overgrown courtyard and onto a side street. Various mini-cars jockeyed for a maze of positions making chaos in our linear minds. People jammed the sidewalk selling candies, hurrying to unknown appointments, and clambering onto overstuffed busses that brushed to the curb. No building in the area was taller than two stories, including our hotel, El Embajador, which had blue adobe arches, black iron balconies and sweeping, paned windows. To our right, the side street intersected a tree-lined boulevard, Avenida Colón. No architectural form dominated the area: a walled colonial home on the other side of the street, a modern cube across the boulevard, then an open field occupied by cardboard and stick huts.

"Sure is a strange place, isn't it boys?" Beef bellowed over our dazzled heads. "You don't suppose this is the center of downtown?"

"No, no, Beef," Emil rolled his eyes. "I was chatting with a fellow in the hotel who said the old centro is a couple of miles that-a-way and I bet we could just grab one of these busses and go have a looksee."

"So," I jeered him, "you going to ask someone in Spanish which bus to take?"

"Hey!" Beef grabbed my shoulder. "Why don't we go ask that cop up there in the traffic stand?"

"Oh, no problem old boys," Emil assured us. "I've had years of Spanish. I'll zing us right through this adventure with no problem at all."

Having studied four years of Spanish, I figured I could handle the situation myself, so I confronted a passerby with, "Perdón, perdón." But he just gave me a confused glare and hurried by.

Emil chuckled, declaring, "You guys don't know Spanish! I'm asking that police fellow." With that he dashed a block up the boulevard to a blue uniformed officer in mid-intersection. Beef and I followed, zipping across vacant lanes, approaching the blue uniform from the rear.

We were within reach, formulating our question, when he raised a white-gloved hand, swung his other arm in a wide arc and simultaneously about-faced on his heels. Traffic was everywhere, bearing down from all angles. It took us by surprise. Dodging cars, we shouted our question at the human traffic signal. He waved and kicked and grew red in the face until we retreated to the sidewalk and decided to take whichever bus came along first.

It was the right bus going the wrong way, which we discovered after we paid our fare and watched the bus slowly empty. At the end of the line we paid another *sucre* and rode back past our hotel towards the colonial center of the city and the bench on which we now sat.

Solitary indications of beauty and harmony flowed onto that bus. Boarding colors and pleats traced cultures that have survived in these lands of the sky for an eon of suns and moons and stars and universes.

Older men, slender and drawn, with gray hair and drab clothing first filled the empty seats. Then, as the bus turned south onto another major thoroughfare a variety of people entered through the folding door. Laborers loading material onto the bus exuded an aura which hinted at lives removed from mountain sanctuaries of harmony and tranquillity to existences of poverty and humility in Quito. Large women, rounded and bustling; I remember one in particular: old and bent with a bulging waist and wearing a soft brown derby. Over her shoulders a heavy wool shawl covered a white linen blouse. Below the waist a light-weight skirt reached to bare, inward twisted feet of tough leathery skin and large deformed toes. On her back she hefted a fifty-pound bag of grain, which she plopped beside our driver before retrieving another that she had left on the street. Brute force, physical labor, people without machines. Behind her came two young men carrying sacks of flour — one hundred pounds each. Harnesses, fit over their foreheads, held loads low on their backs as they trudged up the steps. They were a shorter, stouter people than ourselves, yet I wondered at their strength and physical endurance, as they must have wondered at our oversized frames and looming bodies.

We gave them an exhibition of our giganticism a few blocks further on, past a park, where the boulevard divided into narrow lanes of aging, white adobe structures and we decided to get off before floating further into the unknown. WHAP! Beef's head smashed against the top of the exit as the staring Ecuadorians burst into a round of chortles at the strange foreign personages in their midst.

Down a slope the bus disappeared into a great, white-walled, three-story, colonial city of red-tiled roofs, blue trim and fancy, grilled balconies. We continued on foot along crowded sidewalks, enveloped in a cacophony of babbling sounds. We strolled past dusty windowed shops and great vaulted doors before coming upon a store whose entire front opened onto the street. Within, beads and dusty objects crammed every corner. We ventured in, browsing with wonder at ancient ceramics and aged brass goods. To the rear, dangling heads shrunken to the size of tennis balls with long black hair and peering eyes, caught our attention. Beef, swinging one in hand, turned to Emil asking, "What do you make of this old boy?"

As he examined it closely, a look of astonishment slowly grew on Emil's face. "Hell, Beef, this is the real thing! Look at that hair. And that's dried skin for sure."

Surprised Beef protested, "Oh, bullshit! You can't give me that crap! This isn't a real shrunken head. Get off that stuff."

"Oh now Beef, I wouldn't be too sure about that. There are people out in the Amazon, just east of here, who still practice that cannibalism and shrinking head stuff."

Shaking his own head with a look of disbelief and eyeing Emil warily he said, "I ain't that back hills. I know more than you're giving me credit for. No one is selling real shrunken heads in some tourist shop in Quito. Get off of that stuff!"

"Sure they do Beef," Emil insisted. "A batch of missionaries were eaten up out in the Oriente just a few years ago. Hey, this ain't Iowa. They do some incredibly strange stuff around here."

"Well, that may be, but I'll bet you five bucks this ain't no shrunken head."

"I don't want to take your money, big boy, but if you want to give it away, it might as well be mine."

With confident defiance Beef shook his hand and the bet was on. Emil carried the head through the maze of aisles as Beef and I tailed along behind.

An aging man at the counter smiled as we approached. Bowing slightly he greeted us, "*Buenas tardes señores. ¿Cómo están?*"

At least we all knew what that meant and replied in our best high school Spanish, "*Bien, muy bien.*"

Then, however, the shopkeeper launched into a friendly chat common in Quito: *"Entonces, ¿cómo les va aquí en Quito? ¿Están paseando? ¿Cómo les parece la ciudad?"*

Now we were lost. What was this guy saying? How did we get here? How were we ever going to get back and who was going to answer our questions about this crazy shrunken head?

Emil took the initiative. Swinging the head he peered intensely at the friendly fellow and asked, *"Señor, señor, ¿es real?"*

No luck, he merely stared at us and offered a price *"Cien sucres."*

"No, no, no," Emil persisted shaking his head,

"Hey, hold it," Beef interjected. "This guy just said he was selling this for one hundred *sucres*. That's four bucks. There is no way he is going to sell a real shrunken head for four bucks."

"How do you know that?"

"He said 'cien sucres.' *Cien* is one hundredand a *sucre* is worth four cents. That means four bucks and if this thing is real it's worth a lot more than four bucks. If it's real I'll buy a carload of 'em and ship em back to the States." It was a prophetic statement from someone who ended up exporting Latin American handicrafts back to the States, but it did not quite settle the problem at hand.

Sensing doom, Emil kept up his patter. Holding the shrunken head in his hand, he pointed at it and then at his own head making a shrinking, sucking gurgling sound in his throat. Tugging at his own skin he then pulled on the skin of the shrunken head.

Finally understanding, the man laughed. *"No, no es humano. Hacen del puerco, oink oink oink oink. Para los turistas, no más."*

Made of pig skin for the tourists — so much for Emil's ideas. But as he always said with a sly grin, "What you don't know, you make up."

With Beef beaming from his victory, we continued downhill past more shops and crowded walks, past the old colonial Sucre Theater with its yellowing walls and towering arches. Gawking at our environs, we tramped up Calle Guayaquil into the Plaza de Santo Domingo, where we bought beers through a street-side window and found this ancient bench to rest our legs.

We were in an old stone plaza and *Generalísimo* Sucre, Ecuadorian liberator from Spanish domination, gallantly rode his stone steed above a gurgling fountain at its center. At one time he must have been the featured attraction of this plaza but now he functioned as the divider of a busy, exhaust-engulfed traffic circle. Cars rattled over the rounded stones without giving the long-gone general a thought. He had succumbed to a new invasion.

Across from us on the east side of the plaza the mammoth Santo Domingo Church, convent and monastery arched across streets and blocked off others. Below it people gathered awaiting buses, while in the dazed eyes of occasional street people life lurched by.

On the north side, a collection of small-time bubble gum, sunglass and belt merchants were closing wooden stalls and making street-side beds beneath the overhang of a colonial building. On the other two sides shops dotted the street and in the south-eastern corner, vehicles exited through a curved tunnel onto Calle Rocafuerte and the old neighborhood of La Loma where I lived in the coming weeks.

An added attraction, as we sat on the bench, were the revelers of *El Día de los Reyes*. People dressed in masks and costumes flitted around the plaza. Of course, in our confusion we couldn't distinguish the costumes from the standard dress; it was all exotic to us.

Finishing our beer, we confronted the task of returning to our hotel. We had no idea how to get back. Emil remembered the name of the hotel; Beef remembered the bus had been called the Colón Camal and I spotted one headed in the direction from which we had come. Returning our beer bottles to the vendor we dodged across the plaza to the bus stand and caught the next blue Colón Camal headed north. Exhaustion was upon us, but the anxiety of finding our way back to our beds kept us alert. We wound and twisted through streets we had never seen. Our concern mounted as darkness fell upon the city. Relief came only when we spotted the blue walls of El Embajador and exited the bus on the same side street from which we had set out. Back we went to the soft, white linen of our rooms and a secure rest in preparation for further adventures in an unknown world.

Media
Madness

A WEEK LATER I passed back through the Plaza de Santo Domingo and rode beneath one of the great arches of the Santo Domingo Church into the old barrio of La Loma. Riding with René Salgado and his brother Jaime in René's red Volkswagen bug, I was destined for the Salgado home deep within the mud walls of this old neighborhood where I would live for the next two months.

Heading up Calle Rocafuerte, we parked on the street and passed through a thick wall by way of a wooden gate set within another gate five times its size. This led to a small courtyard of hanging clothes and frolicking children with dark olive skin and fat round faces. Doors on all sides led to crowded quarters and an opening at the end passed to another patio, filled with more clothes and children playing. These houses dated from the era of the colonial Spanish government. A grand catacombed cavern of residences, it was a mass of abodes, one below, several in front, houses to the sides and behind. Mud, straw, plaster, sun, fire and water all held the seventeen-inch thick walls in a solid block.

On the far side of the inner patio, we entered a dark twisting tunnel leading to the Salgado's rear patio and stairs to the back door. This ancient Ecuadorian home forced my senses to grasp the distinction between my new reality and my childhood home in suburban Portland. Dampness pervaded thick adobe and moldy odors and chill entered my pores. Pastel green chips of paint, curling beside a deteriorating china closet revealed earlier coats of pink and yellow beneath. Old family belongings cluttered every corner. Four boys slept in one room, the parents in another. A twelve-year-old servant slept on a tiny cot amidst a stockpile of assorted odds and ends. The next room was mine! Enclosed on all sides, no light entered from the sun, leaving it permanently immersed in gloom. Dark and depressing, it made me sneeze and eventually forced me to evacuate to tiny quarters on the roof.

Water was available only a few hours a day; toilet waste of eight inhabitants collected in one bowl until the sun had fallen and water was restored, leaving a noxious smell floating out of the toilet and down the hall for most of the day. Hot water existed on Saturdays, and electricity often didn't exist at all.

Rain, in torrential downpour, sheeted across the red-tiled roof of the Salgado home on my first afternoon there. René, his wife Bertha, brother Jaime and I all sat around the large dining room table. This cubicle was more table than room and movement by one of its occupants required movement by all. Windows were glazed. A stench of *kerex*, kerosene, white gas or some other combustible oozed from the crusted kitchen, assaulting my nostrils and nauseating my stomach. Four young male Salgados scooted in and out of the room, while the prepubescent Indian servant came when called and otherwise peeked out the kitchen door. They did not seem a wealthy family, though by Ecuadorian standards they were. René worked several jobs as an English instructor in scattered local high schools. Jaime was a trader in whatever there was to trade. Bertha raised the four small ones and ran a street-side stationery store. For them it was a sumptuous house. It was not theirs, but René's father's; the two brothers were raised here. Their father, a tailor of fine men's clothing, had gone off to the States where he labored in a factory of rapid electric looms. Other Salgados had followed, three sons and their only daughter. Off to the Disneylandia of the North, produced by Hollywood, presented by General Motors and distributed by television, movies, magazines and newspapers everywhere.

Back in Ecuador, on the equator, the sun rises and sets at six, regulating all life beneath it, and my life in the Salgado home followed a pattern as regular as the sun.

Shinshi, the maid, twelve years old with long, straight, black hair and dark, rounded features of the indigenous people, was the first to get up. She went to the corner store for fresh bread and milk. By the time I rose a half hour later, the whole family was well into their morning activities. Boys ran in the hall collecting necessary school items. On the dining room table a glass of green *naranjilla* juice, a soft-boiled egg, *café con leche* and fresh bread greeted me.

René, stout and muscular with close-cropped hair, sat at the end of the table munching his breakfast and reading the morning paper. He checked off his boys as they left for school and then left soon behind them.

I followed next, off to language training, out the door by seven-thirty and down to the Plaza de Santo Domingo. There I joined the throngs and caught a Colón-Camal bus across town. Everyone in Quito travels by bus. Once it is mastered a passenger can utilize this brilliant system to travel anywhere in the city or the countryside.

Bertha stayed in the neighborhood. She was a tall woman with broad legs and a sturdy body. Her facial profile was classic: high forehead, arching brows, gently sloping nose, rounded cheeks and a slightly protrusive chin. Her morning was spent caring for Didee, the baby, a chubby, long-haired tike whom she took marketing in a series of shops down Calle Rocafuerte where she bought fresh produce and meat from the same vendors every day.

At noon, the whole family came back: René from work, the kids from school. They stayed two hours to share *almuerzo*, the biggest meal of the day — a large bowl of soup and a plate of rice, meat, vegetables and beans. Then siesta; they took a short rest to digest the food and the day's activities. At 2:30, a second beginning, a new awakening; René went back to work and the kids went back to school.

I was on a shortened American schedule and was home by four, when I usually found Bertha in the cubbyhole stationery store. Sometimes I chatted with her and learned the vocabulary of the stationery business. Other times I retreated to my rooftop quarters. There I would rest or read and be served tea, bread and jelly by the attentive Shinshi.

Patter and pounding of feet and joyful bodies in the hallway below announced the return of the young ones. Crashing and smashing, they chased back and forth in the narrow corridor — another reason I was now living on the roof. A thunder of noise, and then a new sound, a new phenomenon: television.

Just before dinner, I'd saunter down the hall to visit the boys during their viewing time. Sometimes they had the TV in their own room, a long, sleeping space divided by a curtain. Two cots hugged the thick walls, barely leaving a passage to reach two tiny beds behind the curtain. All about clothes and childhood artifacts were strewn among boxes on the floor and shelves on the walls.

Most times, however, the television was across the hall in their parents' bedroom, a more spacious area with slightly more light entering curtained windows. Santiago, nine years into life, lengthy black hair, the oldest brother, a mischievous smirk covering his face, sat on rumpled bed covers. William, "Billy," next in line, sat at his feet, his rear resting on a pile of musty clothes. Stretched out lengthwise was Junior, René the second, named after his father at his birth four years earlier.

For centuries, kids had gamboled about with their neighbors in the outdoor patios of this residential catacomb. Laughing, screaming, hearing, feeling, chasing, smelling, touching; in most parts of this old city kids still spend their afternoons with these activites. But up in this bedroom, draped with loose clothes on open closet doors, these youngsters watched a boob tube full of an industrialized world gone mad on consumption.

Daadt-daadt-daadt-daadt, daadt-daadt-daadt-daadt, daadt-daadt-daadt, daa-da-Botmon, daadt-daadt-daadt-daadt-daadt-daadt, BOTMON. Out from their super duper bat cave, far below their fancy, frilly mansion streamed the masked hero and his leotarded young assistant in their finned-out, gimmicked-up, chopped-off Batmobile. Out to do battle with the schizoid wonderama mass of mechanically-oriented, media-mad monsters, the Joker and others.

Media Madness

Juiced-up, plugged-in, electrolyzed US TV programs in manual, harmonious, physically conscious Ecuador — a strange thing. Programs made in the States, dubbed in Spanish and tuned in by whoever has a television set.[1] Don't have to read, don't have to think, can't smell, can't touch, can't experience objects that happen inside the tube. Here it is folks, everything you ever wanted or could ever want to want from a world crazier than Buck Rogers or Star Wars. But you can't have it, you can only see it and hear it.

Besides Batman, there was Yogi Bear in a land where there were no bears and no national parks for that matter, "I Love Lucie" and a host of other rerun, US productions. In addition to blatantly Americanized programs there was also, every five minutes, advertising.[2]

"Mom, Dad, kids, are you oppressed and downtrodden? Here, be better than everyone else; go out and buy this shiny new whichamadeely. You obviously don't need it or you would already know about it. But, why not go and buy it anyway?" Or — even better — "Here, are you dragged out and bored with life? Get this and you also get the hot sexy model standing next to it and the 40,000 acres of beautiful meadow, canyon and forest just on the other side."

What effect did this mesmerizing have on three pairs of youthful eyes? Cracked and shattered plastic toys littered the antique hallway. The kids wouldn't talk to me when I went in to see them: their eyes glued to the set. I'd trip on the half-destroyed playthings as I left the room. They wouldn't talk to me when they were reading Donald Duck comic books, either. But they probably didn't want to talk to anyone then. Donald Duck comic books never had much good to say about anyone who did not live in the good old *"ooo-ese ahh"* (USA) and none of these kids lived there, that was for sure.

---

[1] Media critic Alan Wells points out that "ABC (owner of the three major television stations in Ecuador through its Worldvision Department) can sell Batman to an advertiser and then place Batman along with designated commercials in any Worldvision country where the advertiser wants it to appear."

[2] Major US networks have been able to convince most third World governments that commercial television is "free" and thus the best way to go. This has led to American formats designed by US broadcasting corporations in most of Latin America. ABC operates in 16 South American countries using 64 transmitting stations. Broadcasting corporations, owned by larger US production units — GE, Gulf Western, Paramount, etc., — have an identifiable interest in promoting commercial advertising and consumerism throughout the world.

Down the hall, at 7:30, René dragged in for a bite of dinner after his day classes and before teaching night courses. Bertha served us a small meal of meat, rice, vegetables and beans. She talked of an electric frying pan that she had seen on the soap operas and wanted to buy. René moaned. I gazed into the kitchen at the kerosene stove, the propane stove and the old wood cook-stove, and wondered where she was going to put it.

René had also been taken in by American movies with flashy cars and what he called "foxy ladies." This fascination was exemplified by his red Volkswagen bug. Here was as useless an item in bus-packed Quito as Bertha's electric frying pan would have been in her stove-laden, servant-filled kitchen.

The hassle of René's car was etched in my mind one evening when I accompanied him and his brother to a soccer club meeting. His car was good for riding, but unfortunately wouldn't start.

On the night of the soccer club meeting, he had parked on Calle Rocafuerte facing downhill. Once the brake was released, the motor coughed and purred into action.

"Hey René," I asked, "how come we're taking the car? The meeting isn't far; we could walk or take the bus."

"O' Jimmy, it's fun to take the car," he smiled with his chubby cheeks bulging out. "Don't worry, I got it fixed," his eyes twinkled. "You won't have to push it."

Down we rolled through empty, twisting streets, tires thumping on the cobblestones. We parked uphill from the meeting — to allow for a running start. Jaime had come in his own car and we joined him inside for the ceremonies.

After the speeches Jaime and René, wanting to visit one of their haunts for a little beer, cards and whatever they could pay the bar girls to provide, climbed into René's Volks. I joined them and René put the car in gear, pushed in the clutch and released the brake. We started rolling. He let out the clutch, brmph . . . brmph . . . brmph.

"Hold it! Stop! Let's look at the engine before we get to the bottom of the hill." René stopped and Jaime jumped out, dashed to the back and threw up the hood. It was dark, the streetlights didn't work, everyone had gone to bed. Jaime couldn't see anything. He plunged in his hand, pulled a few hoses, rattled a few wires and hopped back in.

"OK, let's go; it'll start now."

René put it in gear, released the brake. Rolling again, clutch out, brmph . . . brmph . . .baarmph . . . brmph . . . baarmph, baarmph . . . brmph . . . With the bottom of the hill looming in front of us, René stopped and asked with a sheepish grin. "Well, should I keep going?"

"Sure," Jaime exuded, "go ahead, it almost started."

"Might as well," I said, "I can walk home."

In gear, clutch in, brake off, rolling, brmph . . . brmph . . . barmph, baarmph, baaarrrmmmpph-h-h. We came to a stop, bottom of the hill, still no power. Everyone was gone. Quito was asleep, dead in the night.

"What'll we do now?" I asked.

"Damn, it almost started," Jaime shook his head. "Why don't we try pushing it back up a little ways and do it again?"

"Let's look at the engine first." René pulled open the back, peered into the blackness. "Can't see much." He stuck his hands in, got them greasy and conferred with Jaime. They looked in again, did something and closed the top.

"Come on Jimmy, we're going to try it again. We just have to push it uphill a little bit"

So we all pushed, Jaime on the left headlight, me on the right, and René on the door, steering through the window. "Oooof," it slowly began to roll backwards. Up we went, little by little, weaving around the street, which became steeper and the pushing harder. We couldn't go any further. We were stuck. René couldn't reach the brake. The weight was coming down on Jaime and me. We stepped aside, letting the car roll free before it crushed us. René dove through the window grabbing at the hand brake. I dodged René's dangling feet as they sailed by. Luckily he reached the brake before crashing into any obstacles.

René's furry head rose above the seat. His eyes were beaming, still laughing. He sat up, tried to start it again, no go. Jaime and I joined him at the bottom of the hill.

"Why don't we leave it here," I suggested, "and go home with Jaime?"

"No," René worriedly shook his head, "I don't want to leave the car here."

"I can bring my car around," Jaime offered, "and tow you over to my house."

Jaime got his car, a green machine, a Fiat with a customized cardboard and plywood body. At least it ran. That was all it did. Connected to the Volkswagen, the Fiat wouldn't move, couldn't pull the Volks up the steep hill. With René and me pushing, it did pull it, just barely.

Slowly we pushed the Volks up the deserted Calle Mananbi, onto Calle Guayaquil and into the Plaza de Santo Domingo. René and I dodged cars that still roamed the Quito night. Beyond the Plaza we rode downhill past the Ministry of Defense. René both laughed and swore about his automobile. At the bottom, where the Avenida Oriental, one of Quito's only freeways came in, we had to push again. A uniformed policeman scowled from his traffic box.

Up a long winding gully, cars honked and people yelled as we slowed the cars behind us to a crawl. A sprinkle of rain started to fall. René started to sing. Leveling off at Camal circle, we followed it around, leaving the highway and the irate motorists. A last ascent past the old slaughterhouse took us to the left and Jaime's yard and garage.

I was cold and exhausted and wanted to go home. Saying good-bye, René and I walked to the street. Broad, bright headlights moved down the hill. René stuck out his hand and a familiar blue Colón-Camal bus slowed to let us board. A savior, a straight run to the Plaza de Santo Domingo and our home.

Why own a car in this crazy country? No mechanics, no parts, no tow trucks. Too much American TV, too many Hollywood movies.

Acción Cívica

Around on a path
  that connects at both ends
On a continuing circle
  one continually bends
Battling a foe that's
  infested within
Attacking a problem
  that begins as it ends

fEBRUARY 1972. Tanks in the palm trees of Independence Plaza. The President, José María Velasco Ibarra, is ousted for the fourth time. Ibarra, "The Old One," elected to the Ecuadorian Presidency five times (1933, 1944, 1952, 1960 and 1968), completed his term only once. Four times the military removed him from the presidential palace.

Exploration and discovery by American companies of Amazonian oil wreaked havoc in Ecuadorian politics. Velasco Ibarra volunteered to resign and call for elections. Instead, the young colonels in the military took over, adopted a liberal constitution and declared the establishment of the Nationalist and Revolutionary government under a military junta headed by Generalísimo Guillermo Rodríguez Lara. Previously Lara had been an engineering instructor. Now he was *EL PRESIDENTE DE LA REPUBLI-CA.*

"Nationalist and Revolutionary," they were out to cure their nation's ills: oil money to the people, everyone would be rich. Their problem: very few people were very rich and the rest were very poor. Land reform, a logical solution, a way to give the hungry masses access to under-utilized land, increase production and keep people fed has an inherent foe: existing landowners, both domestic and foreign.

To avoid upsetting the landowners, the junta opened up uninhabited, unexplored, undeveloped land and supposedly let the peasants come in and do what they could. In a land settled for centuries in the mountains and along the coast, the government could only open up the land in between — the jungle. Trusting no one else for this delicate task, the military took it upon themselves to show the nation and the country how to save their society. From such auspicious confidence sprang the *Programa Piloto de Desarrollo en el Noroccidente de Pichincha bajo las auspicias de Acción Cívica de las Fuerzas Armadas*.

January 1973, I entered upon the scene. My purported job, small business advisor, never had, never did and never would exist. Three months later, still clumsy in conversational Spanish and woefully naive in the ways of Ecuadorian politics and money, I was enlisted along with another American, Roberto (Bob) Ladine, as an economist for the Pilot Program of Development of the Nationalist and Revolutionary Government in the Northwest of Pichincha Province under the auspices of the Civic Action Group (Acción Cívica)* of the Armed Forces.

Past the Plaza de Santo Domingo, Quito opens from tight colonial quarters into rolling Andean hills. There, resting on sloping ground separated from the main road by a block of gardens and trees, sat the Ministry of Defense. Beyond the flowers, a long, whitewashed mud wall allowed visitors to enter only through a central gate. Two guards, in what appeared to be used US army uniforms made-over with Ecuadorian insignias, listened to our stumbling Spanish before allowing us to enter.

In front of us stood the Ecuadorian equivalent of the Pentagon, an

---

* Acción Cívica had its beginnings ten years earlier in 1962. Those were the days when the US Alliance for Progress was getting under way as the liberal reform answer to Fidel Castro's revolution in Cuba. Acción Cívica was formed by the US Military Assistance Command in Ecuador as an experimental model counter-insurgency group to work with civilians. Over one million US dollars went into the establishment of Acción Cívica.

antique adobe-brick structure in the mountain tradition. Tall enough to enclose four full floors, it contained only two. Both sides extended fifty yards from a central archway. Under the arch, we mounted a grand double staircase to the upper story and followed an open passage to the left. At the corridor's end, plastered against the wall, a huge yellow and red poster proclaimed the Nationalist and Revolutionary government and how it was out to change the world. To the left, beside the poster, through tall double doors, we found a room cluttered with desks, secretaries, messengers and military personnel. Tucked under the only window sat a close-cropped, kinky-haired civilian. Roberto pointed him out as Oswaldo Berni, hired head and sole employee of the Pilot Program in the Northwest of Pichincha. Round and stubby, he rose when he saw us and began by addressing my cohort, Roberto Ladine. "Good morning Roberto, welcome back to Acción Cívica, I am very glad you're here."

"Oh, and I am glad to be here," Roberto replied, his blond, blue-eyed smile stretching from ear to ear. "I would like you to meet a fellow countryman of mine I told you about, James Tarbell, who could also work on this development project of yours."

"With much pleasure, James," pronouncing my name more like Zhamez, he pumped my hand and continued, "it will be good to have you with us; I am glad to have you here. But first, before he gets away, allow me to introduce you to Major Aguirre, Director of Acción Cívica. Follow me."

We did, to the desk of a young, attractive secretary with whom Oswaldo chatted briefly. She rose and invited us through a closed door of opaque glass to her right. Within this small office crowded with a desk and two chairs, two men were conversing. One, tall and angular with a thin nose and black-rimmed glasses, stood behind a desk covering the receiver of his telephone with his hands while carrying on a brisk discussion with the other, a short, stocky civilian whose back was to us. The major gave us a perplexed glance and with a wave indicated that we wait. With another wave he excused the other fellow and then hunkered down in his chair, swiveled away from us and spoke rapidly into the mouthpiece.

His gray uniform stretched tight, in a moment he gave a thoughtful glance out the window, then swiftly turned to where we stood. "Sí, Señor Berni, what can I do for you?"

"Mi Mayor, I would like you to meet two Americans who are eager to

"You're just what we're looking for. Isn't that right Oswaldo?"

work with us out in the Northwest of Pichincha, Economista Ladine and Economista Tarbell." Then, turning to us he said, "Señores, el Mayor Aguirre, Director de Acción Cívica."

We shook the Major's hand as a gleeful smile spread over his face and his eyes darted back and forth between us. "Gentlemen," he said, "I am so glad to have you with us. We need your help badly on this project. You're just what we are looking for. Isn't that right Oswaldo?"

"Sí," Oswaldo immediately returned, "sí, mi Mayor."

"Gentlemen," the Major went on, "this is a very important project. For the good of the country we must develop this zone. This is the Pilot Program, isn't that right Oswaldo?"

"Sí, mi Mayor, the pilot project."

"And, gentlemen, after we show that we can develop the Northwest of Pichincha we can spread throughout the country."

"We are ready to help," Roberto assured him with a grin.

"Good!" said the Major. "So, are there any questions?"

"I have a quick question," I interjected. "What exactly do you mean by develop? Is your goal to integrate this part of the jungle into the rest of the Ecuadorian economy and society?"

"Precisely," he responded with a bounce. "*Integrate*. That is the exact word the sub-secretary used this morning."

A young man with tousled hair and baggy trousers burst through the door. "*Perdón, mi Mayor*," he exclaimed, "but mi Coronel gave me this note for you and told me it was important." With that he handed a small scrap of paper to Major Aguirre,

"Excuse me gentlemen," and the Major read the note quickly. Stretching his head back towards the ceiling, he gave a slight chuckle and then turning to us said, "I have to leave for a moment; Oswaldo can tell you about the rest of the project, but I hope we can talk more later." Pulling a flat gray hat banded with a bright red braid from its peg on the wall, he stepped swiftly from behind his desk and brushed by us through the door.

Oswaldo Berni exited next, leaving Bob and me to tag along behind. We followed him back to this desk where he began unrolling a great sheath of paper. "My friends," he declared, "this is a map of the zone."

Flattening the scroll on top of his crowded desk, he used a pile of books to hold down one end of the map and a heavy ash tray for the other. Before us spread a blue-printed array of squares and squiggles. Down the middle ran a particularly heavy line and on either side of it various sized geometric shapes and quadrangles were plotted and numbered, filling most of the paper. Bordering the top and bottom was a pair of light curving lines. Names, dots, and details filled in the rest of the sheet. I couldn't understand even part of it.

After surveying it for a few short moments, Oswaldo launched into a lengthy explanation, of which I could decipher only a few portions. "The Provincial Government is putting a road through here," he told us, indicating the heavy central line. "This is where it comes from Quito, rises over the last range of mountains and drops down here to Los Bancos." I missed what he said about this little town and caught him again as he explained, ". . . road is completed to this point, kilometer one thirty-two" — he was pointing to a spot two-thirds of the way across the page — "and they need to cut another twenty kilometers through the jungle before meeting the coast road." Then I lost him until he began swinging his arm around the entire map saying, "everything between Río Guayllabamba on the north and Río Blanco, here on the south," running his pudgy finger along the lines on the top and bottom of the page.

He apparently thought we understood his entire discourse because he plunged on with a defiant smile. "Three hundred fifty thousand hectares [about 1482 square miles] mostly of uninhabited jungle. Only three towns existed out here before the road came through. Mindo, up near the base of the mountains. Pachijal, up here on the Pachijal River, in the middle of the jungle, was settled maybe a hundred fifty years ago by colonists. Before the road came through, it was about a twenty-four hour walk to the nearest town. This is the third town, down here near the coast, Puerto Quito. It's a collection of shacks belonging to some blacks who have always made dugout canoes and floated them to the coast to sell. Those people are pretty surprised by our road coming in behind them. They don't like it a bit. Most of them are picking up everything and moving further into the jungle.

"All these squares here are cooperatives established through the Institute for Land Reform and Colonization. People have been moving in along the road as it's being built and are trying to cultivate the land. I am a founder of one of the biggest co-ops out in the zone. This one here, near Kilometer One Thirteen where Acción Cívica is putting in its community house. Friends from Quito joined me in buying and forming the co-op."

"Oswaldo," Bob asked enthusiastically, "are these really strong, functioning co-ops? Are the members moving out there and setting up their own farms and such?"

"Well, you know," Oswaldo smiled knowingly, "most of the people who have moved out there are campesinos, people from the Sierra and the Coast. Sometimes they can find land in the back country, but it's better for them if they stay near the road and work for the land owners there. That way they can get work and earn money; it's really better that way."

"What kinds of projects," I asked, "do you plan to do out there?"

"Why, projects to develop the area of course," he responded. "Besides helping to build the road we are going to help the people get schools and doctors and help them develop the area economically."

Hoping to clarify the situation I asked, "When you say develop, you mean the same thing Major Aguirre did this morning, integrate the area into the national economy?"

"That's it exactly. Just what the Major was saying. Integrate the whole area into the national life. That means economically, politically and socially. Look, there's great economic potential for the entire zone. I have a report here saying there are one-hundred and forty-two different types of trees out there. A Japanese company is interested in buying all the lumber. I've seen clay along the side of the road we could use to set up a brick factory, and there are lots of minerals too.

"We're using the entire government, the whole thing. Acción Cívica can do it. Right now we're asking for representatives from all the ministries and agencies. Then through them we'll coordinate all the resources we need to get."

"Have you asked the people out there what they want done?" I queried him, "What they need help with?"

"We're going to set up a committee of the residents of the zone to deal with us later," he assured me. "I know some people who would be great on it."

At this point my mind took off on its own tangent and I began staring at the pale green walls, trying to imagine what the Noroccidente was really like. His project raised questions in my head. Deal with the people later? Cooperatives of bureaucrats? Lumber to the Japanese? It occurred to me that we should do a comprehensive study and plan to really understand the consequences of where this project was headed.

When I suggested the idea of a study, Oswaldo was elated. "That's it!" he said. "That's exactly what we need! How do you think we could do it?"

"Oh, Bob and I could probably figure something out," I said.

"Is that right!" he exclaimed.

"Mm hmm," Bob agreed, "that's what we're here for."

"That's great!" Oswaldo said, "but first we have to develop a system to coordinate all these government representatives."

"I could do that," Bob volunteered, "and Jim could probably do the study."

"Sounds good to me," I said. "I'd love to do a study and plan for the area."

"Excellent, gentlemen! The Major will be very happy."

Life in
Rancho Nirvana

E MIL TOLD ME that Quito sits in an intermontane basin. This small valley was perched on the western side of a broader valley defined by the two parallel ranges of the Andes Mountains. The old city occupies the southern end of this basin, while the northern end was traditionally dedicated to agriculture. Now, to the north, where the colonial architecture disappears, a form of American suburban ticky tacky slinks down the valley and spreads up the hillsides.

Given the opportunity, I chose the suburbs. Not ready to remove myself to a pre-industrial urban dwelling or a remote Andean Indian village, I moved into an apartment in suburban north Quito. I had lived with the Salgados for two months and I was ready to be on my own.

Emil Peterson, impresario extraordinaire, took the initiative to find an apartment a month before we were scheduled to move away from our families. He then convinced Lauren (Lorenzo) Heibner and me to join him in this escape back to suburbia. The "if-you're-happy, we're happy" philosophy of the local Peace Corps Director accepted this alteration without protest and we moved as close to the US as is possible in Ecuador.

To reach our new apartment we passed along the east side of the basin on Avenida Seis de Diciembre, past the American Embassy and rows of large, elegant two-story colonial homes. Beyond Avenida Colón the houses were newer, one story structures and sat on small individual lots. Rather than adobe, these houses were made of concrete or brick covered with plaster. Instead of the traditional gable, roofs were either flat, a slightly-pitched shed or else were made with rounded modern arches. These houses spread out rather than up, with miniature manicured lawns surrounding their exteriors. Most amazing of all was the fact that residents of these northern suburbs had water and electricity twenty-four hours a day.

Americans and wannabe Americans lived in these neighborhoods. The streets were graced by domestic maids, silent neighbors and adobe walls topped with glass shards. Dogs growled menacingly behind iron gates, keeping the uninvited away.

During one stroll I was caught off guard when I heard two boys shouting, "Joey, throw me the ball." Five tow-headed youngsters were playing and yelling in the language of the States. Momentarily I was gone, thousands of miles away, back in suburban Portland. Then shaking my head, and pinching my arm, I watched an empty Quito bus move down the street.

In these neighborhoods lived the Yankee missionaries — religious, diplomatic and economic. From here they dispensed their missionary zeal. Not only did they spread the word of their particular beliefs, but by living the suburban life, they spread the beliefs of the suburban culture.

Youthful advocates of the Church of Latter Day Saints were particularly polished display cases of American culture. They were usually slender examples of Aryan youth: golden hair, blue eyes and well tailored, three-piece suits. Pairs of these young people popped up all over the country — in city streets and country markets they could be seen hawking their wares.

I usually saw them on a bus, but they never seemed to see me. Often as I sat on a rollicking conveyance full of people and music, one of these missionaries would be sitting across the aisle. It was such a great scene that I would try to make contact with them to share this glorious moment. But there was a barrier there that was not to be crossed, at least not by me. With my long hair and casual clothing I was, perhaps, to those Mormon eyes something worse than the heathens they had come to Ecuador to save.

They were, of course, not the only missionaries around. We government types did a notable job of our own, spreading the word of North American society and ways. Those associated with the Peace Corps took cameras and radios to the depths of the jungle, opening up markets with nary a thought.[1] Diplomatic bureaucrats — USAID, embassy staff, etc. — put on a much grander show working hard to open up doors for the global marketplace to enter this land.[2]

The embassy was the temple of this diplomatic mission. Located on a major traffic circle it was an imposing, white, three-story structure occupying most of a block. Great sparkling thick walls, topped with sharp broken glass, enclosed most of the grounds, leaving only the grand entryway open to view. Spear-pointed iron-bar gates insured that the sumptuous courtyard, with its eagle-in-stone and black limousines, would not be violated by passing Ecuadorians.

Around the backside, on a narrow street, Ecuadorians entered through a single door in an otherwise blank wall. This was the consulate where they came — often in vain — to seek visas. It was usually crowded, like some driver's license bureau, everyone seated in bright plastic chairs. Pasted on the walls were gaily colored posters of huge US cities, Disneyland and other such dreamlike attractions.

Back in North Quito just such an attraction was sprouting in the fields of the valley bottom: El Comercio Central, the Commercial Center, a mall

---

[1] President John F. Kennedy, Peace Corps' initial benefactor, didn't miss the point when he said, "Too little attention has been paid to the part which an early exposure to American goods, skills and American ways of doing things can play in forming the tastes and desires of newly emerging countries." (NYT, 9/18/63)

[2] Eugene R. Black, former Chairman and President of the World Bank pointed out that, "our foreign aid programs constitute a distinct benefit for American business. Three major benefits are (1) they provide a substantial and immediate market for US goods and services, (2) ithey stimulate the development of new overseas markets for US companies and (3) they orient national economies toward a free enterprise system in which US firms can prosper. (Columbia Journal of World Business, Fall 1965.)

— concrete and asphalt — born of the single home and private auto boom that was enveloping this end of the valley.

Most of the customers came in their own cars and parked in the asphalt lot. I had to walk because no major bus line went there. When I walked, I could just make out the white walls of the mall from Avenida Seis de Diciembre. Wandering along a muddy trail — there were no sidewalks, everyone drove — I passed Colegio Cotopaxi, the American High School. This was one of four English speaking high schools in Quito, which had no high schools at all for the 40% of the population who spoke Quechua, the ancient language of the Incas. It was to this high school that the offspring of the American missionaries and the Ecuadorian wannabes were sent to learn the ways of North American adolescence, Levis and rock-n-roll.

Just past the gray walls of the high school, the shopping center could be seen across a green rolling field. Looming steel doors gaped open in its brick, rear walls to swallow the goods that were delivered by truck. Small imported autos whizzed down the lane and I could see them parked in straight rows on the flat, black surface beyond. As I approached, the mall grew larger but gained little life, increasing only in concrete and steel.

I entered through La Fuente, an actual soda shop with individual booths and a long ice-cream bar. I used this as a passage to the interior mall, a temperature-controlled corridor of concrete and glass. Neatly groomed customers in slacks and sport shirts strolled through a half dozen shops.

Lounging students from the Colegio Cotopaxi hung out in "MacDonalds" slurping chocolate shakes and stuffing down burgers. Across the way a toy shop displayed thousands of plastic items through its glass window. Farther on were drug and clothing stores and at the end a massive supermarket, La Favorita.

I typically bought more items than I could comfortably carry. So, stymied by the lack of buses, when it was time to go home I joined the suburban masses and used a car — I hired a taxi.

It took me out onto Avenida de Los Estadios and east toward our apartment on the hill. Crossing Seis de Diciembre we climbed into a world that might well have been called Rancho Nirvana. This American suburban hybrid was full of short, squat concrete structures without distinguishing features.

Three blocks up, I got out at the home of Licenciado Pérez, his wife and their near-perfect eight-year-old daughter. A god-awful pink color of brick and cement, it was a one-story square structure devoid of any life.

The yard sat several feet above road level and I entered through a locked steel gate. Passing a yelping dog enclosed in the landlord's carport to ward off would-be-intruders, I climbed a few steps to a concrete path that dissected a narrow ten-foot strip of grass in front of the plate glass windows of the Perez home. From here the Pérezes had a fine view through their cyclone fence of the Quito Valley and Mount Pichincha rising thousands of feet above the city. I continued around the corner to the front door of our L-shaped apartment, which ran along the north and back side of the Pérez's one-story pink suburban home.

The Pérezes were a family on the path of the American ideal: the father commuted to a nice job at the Banco Central, they had a fine home in the suburbs and one perfect child. Their lives were much like the movies portrayed life in the States. The perfect addition would have been several American gentlemen living around back, paying a little rent.

Unfortunately for the Pérezes, it was the age of the American hippie, a phenomenon that never appeared in the Batman and Father-Knows-Best reruns on Ecuadorian TV. Being the first of our group to establish our own pad, we became an attraction to other Americans longing for a little independence. People came at all hours of the day and night.

Since our entrance passed in front of the Pérezes picture windows, our visitors were not a secret, and their long hair and ragged clothing did not sit well with our landlords. In addition, we were typical ethno-centric American youth intent upon living our life as we pleased, totally oblivious to the cultural norms around us. Since our space was around back, we needed to be in the front yard to enjoy the sun. Emil often pranced around there in his white-trimmed blue bathrobe that ended mid-thigh leaving his knobby knees and hairy legs open to viewing by whomever entered the Pérezes front yard.

Another quirk of Emilio's was that he didn't have much dedication to the institution that had brought us to Ecuador. We converted *Cuerpo de Paz*, Spanish for Peace Corps, to *Cuerpo de Paseo*, Spanish for "vacation corps." Within weeks Emil took an extended trip to Colombia and brought back many tales of Medellín and huge drug operations. He also brought back some backpacker friends he'd met on the road and he always had an ample supply of female companions.

Lauren Heibner, our roommate, a devout Mennonite and a graduate of a Mennonite College, found this quite remarkable. Raised in Nebraska, he spent much of his youth working at the church packing up supplies so the community could survive judgment day. It was a sober existence: the gas station on the interstate was the most exciting spot in town. He was a skinny guy, about five-foot-nine, with glasses and a mousy mustache. His hair was short and straight and he often wore a tan rain hat to protect himself from the equatorial elements. He acknowledged that Ecuador was a wild adventure for him and I think that Emilio's escapades were as shocking to Lorenzo as they were to the Pérezes.

Lorenzo and I were particularly envious of Emilio's girlfriends. In our odd living arrangement, Lorenzo and I slept in two cubby holes off the kitchen while Emil had somehow claimed the one bedroom with a door. I remember one night as particularly raucous behind that closed door. The next day, after his woman companion had gone on her way, we were sitting around the kitchen table and Emil began to expound on the previous night's activities.

"Oh, you boys," he said smiling, with a twinkle rising in his eyes, "you boys wouldn't believe what I went through last night. Didn't get any sleep. She was rough and she was wild." He paused and looked around at us and we must have been listening with our mouths open, because he just went on with his tale. "We went at it and went at it again and again and she just wanted more and more. By three o'clock in the morning I was exhausted. I just couldn't make her happy, she just had energy that wouldn't quit." Then pausing and eyeing us he continued. "You know what I should have done? I should have sent her out here to you boys. Ohh," he rolled his eyes, "you would have liked that. Wouldn't that have been a surprise if she'd come crawlin' into bed in the middle of the night and started humping away like mad. Whoooeee! Yep, you boys would have liked that one. Woulda had the time of your lives. Yessireee, I should have done that."

Connections
of Wealth

IANE MORENO, a solitary backpacker from Ventura, California, caught my fancy. Having traveled through South America for several months, she planned to return to the States from Quito. Tall and angular with long dark hair, she was older than I by several years but I always have liked older women. Emil knew I was interested the day he found a note I left informing her that she could sleep "in the living room or anywhere else she wanted."

Nothing came of this except a great friendship until we made a weekend visit to the Otavaleños and their Saturday morning market. Hitchhiking north along the two-lane Pan American Highway on a sunbaked Friday afternoon, we caught a ride with a director of the National Development Bank in a gray Toyota Land Cruiser. We headed out of Quito past forests of spindly eucalyptus and cultivated fields sectioned by rows of cactus. Occasional rammed-earth huts dotted the scene till we reached barren cliffs and descended through dry stone and sand to a rocky river bottom. So went the Andes, great towering mountains and plentiful basins gashed by desolate crevasses carved by waters heading east to the Amazon or west to the Pacific.

In the town of Guayllabamba, we were pulling our bags from the jeep when Diane stuck out her hand and a yellow Toyota sedan stopped to give us a lift. With a wave good-bye to our first ride, we stuffed ourselves and our bags into the back seat of the second. A small auto, it carried a slender, dark Ecuadorian youth and was driven by a much larger man of a lighter hue.

The driver acknowledged our thanks for stopping with a "You're welcome" in unaccented English. He then lapsed into his native Spanish to introduce his fellow passenger and then himself, José Gustavo de Caldillo. His sleeves were short and his pants a light brown. Barely an inch separated a balding head from the black interior roof of his new little car. Keeping to Spanish and twisting his head, he inquired, "And where are you from?"

Joining in the customary friendly banter of Ecuador I said, "We're from the States. I'm living in Quito and Diane here is visiting your country for a short while."

"I've never been to the United States," he told us. "I normally go to Europe. But tell me, how do you like my beautiful country here?"

Out of the village now, speeding along narrow, twisting curves our exuberant driver was only half mindful of thousand-foot cliffs lurking to our left. "I have a farm here," he told us, "this side of Cayambe. I love this area; it's the most beautiful spot in the world."

We made no response and continued in silence, if for no reason than to give the man a chance to keep his eyes on the road. Diane broke the quiet with a question: "What are those small scruffy trees that grow up on the hillside?"

"Those are . . ." he began and then trailed off into an explanation in Spanish that neither of us understood.

"*Perdón, no entendemos*"

"Oh, that's Cerocarpus Breviflorous," he said, amazing us by a switch to flawless English.

"You speak surprisingly good English," I said,

"I speak English, French, German, Italian, Spanish and a little Quechua that the Indians speak."

"Where," I asked in amazement, "did you learn all those languages?"

"Just learned them while I was growing up," he explained. "I don't get much of an opportunity to speak English. But, say, we're coming to my turnoff. Would you two like a spot of tea before continuing on your way? You don't have much more to go."

We pondered the invitation as we slowed for a routine police checkpoint, and as I looked to Diane, she gave a nod of approval.

With our acceptance, José Gustavo de Caldillo said a few words to his other passenger who hopped from the car before the police waved us on.

No longer on bleak hillsides, we entered an area of green fields and distant blue mountains. No crops could be discerned in the broad healthy meadows and wild grasses abounded over a buildingless scene. Contemplating this, I wondered where he could be planning to drink a cup of tea.

As we crested a knoll, the equatorial marker came into view and our driver slowed and turned to the right. On a narrow dusty road, lined by tall eucalyptus, we wound into a valley and up the other side. Through the trees I detected the white walls of *huasipungos*,[1] the homes of the Indians who work on massive estates virtually as slaves.

Around the next corner a building complex came into view. To the right stood a low, one-story adobe ranch home spreading past trees and gurgling fountains. To the left ran a row of larger, whitewashed storage sheds, stables and barns. Farther on, numerous horses grazed in corrals.

"This is my home," our driver informed us, "and if you've got time, I'd like to show you around."

"It's a beautiful spot," we said, staring in disbelief. Then I added, "I'm sure we'd love a tour."

Out of the car, we were drawn to the horses and walked to their corral. "My, those are marvelous animals!" Diane exclaimed.

[1] *Huasipungo* is the name of the small plot of land used by Indian families on large *haciendas*. The Spanish monarchy granted the forebears of these families, along with massive tracts of land to friends of the king. Known as *huasipungueros* these families live on one *huasipungo* for generations with no chance to find another existence. They work on the *hacienda* five or six days a week, at one fifth the already low wage rate. Each man also works as a *cuentayo* or *huasicama* doing special chores from dawn till dusk three months of the year.

Watching, he smiled and nodded his concurrence. "I have forty-five show horses from all over the world, and I have them here for my personal use." Pointing out a light tan horse he said, "This one is a very gentle, highly prized stallion, a true wonder." Turning to Diane, he asked, "Would you like to go for a ride?"

With her delighted assent he signaled a man to saddle the stallion and as Diane mounted, I gazed around in awe. It was a lord's manor from centuries gone by. On all side, huasicamas scurried about.

As Diane rode down the drive at an even lope I asked, "Tell me Señor Caldillo, how long have you lived on this land?"

"Well, I'll tell you young man," he replied, "this whole area has been in my family for six generations. It's part of my soul."

"What kind of crops do you have here?"

"Oh, I've got 700 head of cattle and a thousand acres of wheat. Besides that I've got a little corn, barley and oats."

We watched Diane prance the big steed with gentleness and ease. Then, when she had dismounted, we started our tour. Passing through the corrals, we approached several small bull rings. One was for practice; the other for show. The second was a solid structure of adobe and rock. Several rows of seats surrounded the arena and the walls were a mosaic of the most intricate design. From here he led us to an exotic garden planted with species from around the world. The small pond in its center, José Gustavo de Caldillo informed us in English, "is where my wife likes to go angling. But she doesn't appreciate this climate, so she lives at our home on the coast. My children live in our Quito house, so I am here alone most of the time. But, alas, the sun is setting. Let us return to my house for the tea I have promised."

Twenty thousand foot Mount Cayambe caught our attention as colors from a setting sun cast a pinkish glow on its snow-covered peak. Below the pink snow, greens and blues led to a darkening valley bottom. We were in a feudal land complete with serfs and slaves and a smiling king.

Back at the house, he ushered us through a spacious kitchen to the main sitting room. Long and wide, with thick rough beams and light adobe walls, it had several seating arrangements grouped about its expanse. Chairs pulled next to a flickering fire invited us to a serving table set in white linen.

Once we were seated, a dark, stout fellow garbed in white rolled in a tray of cheese, crackers and tea. "This is my man Alvarez; he's been with me for years."

Alvarez nodded, though the introduction was in English. Taking his gloved hands from the tray, he placed them behind his back.

"This man is a great hunter, very skilled and very quick. He has led me on safaris to all parts of the globe."

We extended our greeting and Alvarez nodded. He then made a slight bow to his master and exited through the door from which he had come.

"Please have a taste of this cheese. It comes from the milk of my cows."

"I certainly shall," Diane said with a smile. "You have been very gracious and we thank you very much. Neither of us has seen a setting like yours before."

"It's a dying breed my dear, and they want to take it away. It's the Americans who are doing it and I don't understand why."[2]

Both Diane and I shrugged more from embarrassment about where we were from than the fact that there were attempts to redistribute these massive land holdings. "It's the coming of new powers and changes," I mumbled in humble reply.

As we sipped our tea, another fellow entered. He too was tall like our host, but rather slender and had a light skin tone as if from a European stock. He walked to our host's chair where they talked quietly and fast, not allowing us to hear. When they had finished, the new arrival rose as if to leave, but José Gustavo de Caldillo laid his hand on the man's arm signaling him to stay.

Turning back to our curious eyes, he made the introduction: "I would like you to meet my foreman, Antonio de Silva."

We rose in greeting, extending our hands and he shook them warmly as we exchanged salutations.

"Antonio comes from Spain. I searched a long time and found him myself. He too comes from a beautiful land of expansive plains. He is a

---

[2] He must have feared the threat of losing it rather than the actual fact, for that rarely happened. Ten years earlier the US Government had included land reform as part of the requirements for aid from the Alliance for Progress. Their formula required that all unused land tracts be broken up, except those belonging to US firms. A politically untenable contradiction, land reform in Ecuador and in the rest of Latin America never effectively took place except in the lightly inhabited jungle like the Northwest of Pichincha Province.

top-flight equestrian, the best I could find. So I imported Antonio and his family to keep my ranch running.

"He is truly a gentleman of the great Spanish tradition. If we ask him nicely, he may recite a little poetry he knows."

Antonio accepted this invitation and, with a light in his sad eyes, sat on the arm of an overstuffed chair. In deep rolling Spanish he asked, "Have you heard of a poet named García Lorca from my country? He combined words very beautifully as I would like to show you now." With that he launched into a verse of deep flowing tones that bounced off the beams and echoed through the room.

Our host joined him in a poetic round of gentle and rich Spanish, and then asked if it wasn't time we continue on to Otavalo. We agreed and thanked him profusely for being so kind. Loaded in his car along with his foreman we drove to the highway as our host and his companion admired a small handgun they kept in the glove compartment. After reaching the highway, Señor de Caldillo chased a bus with his car, passing on the left and forcing it stop so that we could get aboard. We hopped from the car and ran to the waiting transport, still lost in wonder over the afternoon we had spent.

At the bus door, we heard sounds and caught aromas emanating from within. This bus was crammed beyond its limit with this country's beasts of burden. The indigenous peoples, the workers, filled every available inch with their bodies and bundles. Raising our packs above our heads, we squeezed in as best we could and rode the next bumpy hour breathing the bodisome stench of the tightly packed humans. It was a condition our afternoon's host probably never had experienced.

Sweat and toil of the local *indígenas* keep splendid *haciendas* in the style we had just witnessed. Relegated to this role since the time of the Spanish conquest, they rode this bus to the heart of their existence, the Saturday morning market, where they bartered and traded for life's essentials. Our bus deposited us in Otavalo, namesake of the indigenous people that populate the shores of Lago San Pablo.

We lingered in the back of a small bar sipping *hervidos* (cane alcohol and fruit juice) at a wobbly wooden table oblivious to the drinking locals who had come to town for the market. We concentrated on each other and our incredible experience with José Gustavo de Caldillo.

We drank more and later than we should have, because when we stumbled out to find a bus there was none to be found. So we hired an old Chevy taxi and described to the driver where we wanted to go, a shack out by the old abandoned mansion on the far side of the lake where my friend Pat Doherty lived. The driver indicated that he knew where it was. Confident we were on our way, Diane and I fell into a pod in the back seat. As I slipped an arm around her she gave me an engaging embrace and pulled me to her. Locked in torrid fondling, we were oblivious of our driver or locale until he stopped in the middle of a dirt road and announced that he had no idea where we wanted to go.

Rousing myself from our passions, I surveyed the dark and unfamiliar scene and then directed him back a mile or so until I recognized the driveway that headed down to the lake. We paid and thanked him for the ride.

Walking down the drive on a beautiful starry night, we thought it was too late to wake Pat and decided to sleep by the shore. Laying our bags beside each other as the waves rippled on the grassy beach and towering bulks of the Andes rose on all sides, I slipped into my bag and removed my clothes in some anticipation of what was to come. Diane, lying next to me rolled over to give me a good night hug and I pulled her toward me to share the night.

Next morning's sunrise illuminated a serene scene of grandeur and harmony. On one side blue water spread out for a mile to a shoreline of faintly visible trees. From there the ground rose through green fields to the gray craggy heights of massive Mount Mohanda, reflecting the first rays of the day's early light. To the other side, Mount Imbabura rose blocking the sun in twin conal spires of volcanic ash. Far up its side, Otavaleños cultivated land so steep I was surprised they could plow it. All about green grasses enveloped grazing cattle up to their knees. The area was well populated and people could be seen doing their chores, but not a noise could be heard.

Residents trod barefoot through dust and slipped into the lake without a sound. Their work was by hand, their lives simple, without a machine to disrupt their day. They lived in small earthen houses of red clay tile roofs, with no windows or furniture and only a dirt floor. Their families had lived here for centuries, growing corn and potatoes in full view of the ever-present lake and the great looming mountains.

Slipping out of our love nest as the sun crested Imbabura, we walked hand-in-hand to Pat's reconverted adobe shed behind the crumbling lakeside mansion. Patricio had arrived with Emil, Lorenzo, Beef, and myself in the most recent batch of Peace Corps inductees. A stout Irishman, he had insatiable enthusiasm and a driving desire to experience everything.

He was all smiles to see us and fixed a big breakfast as we chatted away. It took so long to get our day going that we missed the morning market and had no reason to desert this beautiful scene. So we walked in the fields and swam in the lake and let the sun dry the skin on our backs.

r r r ra rrrrrRRRROARRRrrr r ra r r r r rrrrrrRRRROARRRRrrrr r r

In the midst of our dreams, peace and placidity, a shattering interruption split the air. From the far end of these traditional waters a speeding motor boat split the tranquil surface, water skier in tow.

"Say, Pat," I asked, "what's that out there?"

Scanning the lake and discerning the small moving boat he replied, "Oooh, that sure is ugly. I've never seen water-skiers out here before."

"Jesus," I moaned, "that's sad. It destroys the entire environment of the lake."

Raising herself on her elbows and shaking her head Diane asked, "Where did he come from?"

"Oh, I think the richies from Quito built a yacht club down here and come on the weekends to play with their boats."

"I wonder how the Indians like that?"

"It must blow them away."

Zooming around in wide circles, the pilot, steering his speedster boat for a nearby pass, waved at our white faces staring out of the grass. We waved in return, watching him zip by and soon he was back, slowing to chat.

"Ahoy there," said the pilot, a young blond of German descent as he slipped his boat onto the bank at our feet.

"What are you folks doing out here?" he asked in slightly accented English.

"I live here," said Pat, "and you, how do you happen to be here with your boat?"

"I belong to a yacht club we just built down the way. I come up on Saturdays to get in a little boating. Would you like to go for a ride?"

Thick American blood rose from our depths. Lust we had learned for speed and power flowed through our veins. Respect we had for local lifestyles was blocked from our minds. We stepped into the boat.

Pat went water skiing as we whipped through the waves. After a quarter of an hour, we docked at the clubhouse and were invited in for a scotch. The building was a modern white ferrocement structure. It had a low, sweeping roof and huge opening windows of solid plate glass. Inside, a carpeted seating area sank below the slate floor. Flames jumped within a heavy stone fireplace on the far wall.

A half-dozen club members in expensive casual garb were quietly milling around the expansive room. As I sat on a couch, I asked a club member what his business was in Quito. He too was a German fellow with shocking blond hair and deep sea blue eyes.

"I run Thomas Bus Works," he told me, "out in Cotocollao, north of town."

"You build all the Thomas buses that run around Quito?"

"No, we just import the parts and assemble them here. The mother company is from your country, from North Carolina. They send us parts and we put them together.

"Is there any way," I continued to question him, "that an Ecuadorian company could manufacture those parts?"

"No, nothing like that goes on in this country. You Americans control all the manufacturing. There's nothing along those lines that Ecuadorians can do."

"You sound more like an American than an Ecuadorian when you talk."

"Well," he responded with a slight smile, "the Americans got a head start in industrialization; now they monopolize it.[3] If an Ecuadorian wants to invest his family's wealth, he's got to work with a foreign firm. There's no choice; multinational corporations, the biggest in the world, are coming in every day and buying local companies. There are raw materials, cheap labor and completely untapped markets. They come in and cart the profits

---

[3] Fifty-eight percent of all firms in Ecuador are foreign controlled, which includes 60% of all commercial enterprises and over 50% of all banking assets. At least 35% of Ecuador's industry is foreign controlled along with 35% of their agriculture. In 1975, there were at least 28 US firms with direct investments worth $41 million operating in Ecuadorian industry.

away. So, it's either do it with the Americans or don't do it at all."

Diane signaled from the far side of the room, so I excused myself and, thanking our host, slipped out the front door. Wandering past the club members' Mercedes, we headed down the dirt road, back to the land of the *campesinos*. I gazed at their tranquil way of life and thought of the disruption that development and consumerism would bring.

After spending another night at Pat's, we headed back to the northern Quito suburbs that were becoming the domicile of the new Americanized wealth. Later that week Diane headed back to the States as scheduled, leaving me alone to deal with the contradictions and confusions that were unfolding in my life.

First Coming

To the depths of the jungle

to make the world ours,

Flying machines and strange white geeks

meet at the appointed hour.

Have the gods arrived? It's all so weird.

What is the meaning of this?

To impress upon minds and vulnerable hearts

that we are the harbingers of bliss?

WE FOUND THE FUEL TRUCK behind mounds of lush green growth, away from the main landing strip beside three high-winged planes of the Ecuadorian Air Force. Grass mingled amongst the wheels of the ancient yellow truck, long stationary, dabs of rust clinging to its bulging sides. Men in drab-green uniforms hopped to the ground from the back of Acción Cívica's brown Chevy pickup. Throwing open the rear steel door of the pump truck, they reeled off a hose in a flurry, flipped switches and pushed the starter, but nothing happened; no engine, no pump, no gas dripped from the nozzle.

Darkness continued to gather. Oswaldo Berni swung his pudgy legs from the cab and walked to the working men.

"Hey, what's wrong here?," he demanded. "We're in a hurry."

"Don't know," one of the privates responded, fiddling with the controls. "It won't start and the instructions are in English."

"Well, find somebody who knows how to run it. We're meeting a helicopter in the jungle tomorrow and we've got to have this fuel with us."

By now our chauffeur, bulky Sargento Jerez, was beside Oswaldo staring at the knobs and dials. Bob and I watched from the bed of the pickup.

"You think we'll ever see the Northwest of Pichincha Province?" Bob asked.

"Don't know," I responded. "It doesn't look like their pump is working. Good thing this crew planned to leave at seven this morning. It has taken ten hours to get to the north end of Quito. At this rate we may not arrive until sunrise. How long a drive do you think it is?"

"Four, maybe five hours."

"Is that to where we are staying?" I asked.

"Don't know, but that is where we're meeting the helicopter."

At this point Oswaldo, Sargento Jerez, three men from the local base, Oswaldo's friend who was riding in the cab and a young man who'd been riding in the back with us, were all crawling over the pump truck in an effort to make it operational. Nothing was working.

Finally Sargento Jerez had the brilliant idea of siphoning the gas out of the pump truck into the barrels in our pickup truck. It was a good idea, potentially ruined because only six inches of fuel remained in the bottom of the truck tank. Luckily it was enough for our purposes.

An hour later, as darkness fell, tanks strapped to the tailgate, with Jerez, Oswaldo and his friend in the cab and Bob, our unintroduced traveling companion and me facing backwards in the truck bed, we were off for our first venture to the Northwest of Pichincha Province.

Climbing up over the shoulder of Mount Pichincha, five minutes above the valley floor, the paved street became rough cobblestones. Ten minutes later it was rutted, stomach-jarring dirt. At ten thousand feet we got cold; at eleven thousand it rained. Bob spread his sleeping bag over our laps. As long as the truck kept moving and we sat pressed against the cab, the rain didn't hit our heads.

Bob turned to our silent traveling partner. "Does it take long to get to Los Bancos?," he queried.

Smiling, the young man replied, "Oh, a long time, we've just begun."

Bob and I moaned.

Noting our dismay our companion reached beneath our covering and produced a tall, slender, reused bottle of clear liquid. "Here, I've got something to help with the trip," he offered.

"What's that?," we both asked.

"*Trago, aguardiente*, pure cane alcohol, the best in the world, they make it out here," and with that he took a long swig. "Here, go ahead; try some."

I knew what it was; I'd drunk it before on stumbling nights in Quito with René Salgado. Nasty stuff, true rot gut booze that burned even before it went down.

I felt the rain, the cold, the darkness, reached for the bottle and took a shot. We all did. Up one mountain and down into a deep valley, backwards, bouncing on a one-lane road, past a town and into blackness. More curves. We couldn't see much. Descending, we were lower than we had been. The air grew warmer; water gurgled; large leafy shadows hung above our heads. Like children we asked, "Are we there yet?"

Handing us the bottle, he shook his head, "Maybe half way."

Hours passed; beyond a lightless junction of grass and wood huts, we climbed once again. The air grew colder, the road rougher, the curves worse, myself more nauseated. When would we reach Los Bancos? We were supposed to be descending into the jungle, but we were again climbing into the mountains. I knew the more we went up, the more we would have to come down.

"This is the last summit," our friend informed us.

"How long until we arrive?" I asked.

"Maybe an hour."

He was optimistic. The first house appeared along the road in one hour, the town in two. Our truck pulled to a muddy halt along a street lined with wood plank structures built in the fashion of the boom-towns of the old American West. Oswaldo Berni, troop leader, twelve hours behind schedule, slid from his seat to bang on a wooden door over which a shaky hand had scrawled, "Residencia Los Bancos." Moments passed before a light shone through the cracks in the walls and a long-gowned woman appeared at the door. Their conversation lasted several minutes, with the woman shaking her youthful head.

Oswaldo returned to the truck. Leaning over the side of the bed he said, "She says we arrived too late. I told her we were coming and needed six beds, but she says now there are only two. Who wants one?"

I quickly volunteered; Oswaldo's friend got the other. He and I followed the waiting woman through the door into a room lit only by a flickering flame held by our guide. We crossed a wood plank floor, past pool tables to a steep, narrow staircase. At the top we continued to the end of a narrow corridor where the lady motioned for us to enter a door to the left. Dim candlelight revealed seven crowded beds filling the simple room. Closing the door, she revealed one more and nodded that it was mine. Tired and cold, I was ready for bed, almost any bed, but I wasn't ready for this: plain hard planks — no mattress, no cushion, just a tattered blanket. Little did I know that in the jungle this is luxury.

Sleep, though, came easily. Sunrise flooded through the street-side windows when my eyes opened. All the beds were empty and only one fellow occupant lingered in the room, fumbling with his clothes. Rolling out of bed, I stumbled to the window for my first inspection of the jungle village of Los Bancos.

One mud strip road traversed the length of the town with brightly colored, false front structures lining it for half a mile in either direction. Behind them hung the encroaching jungle. Horses and trucks slid through the bog created by the previous night's rain. Residents were opening doors and washing faces at an open faucet across the way. Chickens and dogs scratched at their feet. Acción Cívica's truck stood directly below and a smiling Bob Ladine informed me they were going to breakfast in a dingy building opposite my window.

Ten minutes later, as I passed through its doors, it appeared dingier yet. Thick cobwebs hung from the low rafters and hoards of flies stuck to hanging tape strips. Long wooden tables, blue and battered, stood along the walls. Smaller tables filled the middle. None was occupied by my traveling companions. I poked my head through an opening in the rear to see if they were there. It was a smoke-filled kitchen, staffed by two sweating women working over a bubbling black cauldron set on coals. Beside them a man cut vegetables, swatting pea-sized flies from his brow. He was short with big, bulging eyes and jowly cheeks that gave him the appearance of a toad. I asked him if he had seen Oswaldo. He shook his head no.

Retreating outside to search for my friends, I wandered up the street, peering in doors. People stared back. Even people I didn't peer at stared. I became self-conscious before reaching the end of the town and headed back the way I had come. People were still staring. Down I went, past open-air store fronts. Everyone stopped what they were doing to stare or wave. Near the far end of town I spotted a towering blond head through a dark door. It had to belong to an American, to my cohort, Bob Ladine. It did and he truly stood out. Six-foot-five, blond hair and blue eyes in the midst of brown-skinned, brown-eyed black-haired people a foot-and-a-half shorter. Compared to him, I was a side show; he was the main attraction.

I joined Bob, Oswaldo and Sargento Jerez for breakfast. They were a cheery lot considering they only had two hours' sleep and were eating a mournful looking slop. With them sat a lady who was introduced as María Elena, a graying, darkly dressed school marm. She was asking, "Now, Señor Berni, what hour will your helicopter be coming?"

"The sub-secretary told me it would arrive at your school, at eleven o'clock sharp."

"Well," she exclaimed, "if it's eight-thirty right now, that means we have only two and a half hours to prepare."

"No, no," Oswaldo interjected. "I've already talked to the woman who helps you. She is setting up signals on your playground to show the helicopter where to land. So no one has to do anything."

"Oh, but Señor Berni, the whole town is in preparation. We must have a ceremony and you are invited along with the pilots to several special lunches, one up the street at Leonardo's, one over at the Salón de Puerto Quito and one . . "

"No, no, no, Señora," Oswaldo interrupted. "We can't do all of that. We don't have time. They're planning a lunch for us at Kilometer One Sixteen."

"Señor Berni!" she exclaimed. "You can't have lunch there, you must have it here. We are the biggest and most important town on the road. Your lunch should be here!"

"Oh, Señora. We'll talk about it later. Now we have to prepare for the landing." Turning to the woman of the cafe he said, "Quick, bring our bill." Paying, he excused himself from the table and plunged out the door.

María Elena followed, waving her hand, trying again to catch his attention. Bob and I meandered down the street.

"You know where the school is?" I asked him.

"Yeah, we passed it this morning. It's just down this hill."

"Should we take a look?"

"Sure."

Clusters of children collected as we walked down the road. Occasionally, one of their group dashed away to tag our pant legs and return to the giggling cluster. Small boys, no more than five years old, took our hands and in deeply accented voices said, "Hello mister."

A man hailed us from inside an open-air stall. When we didn't stop, he jogged out the door and came to our side. "Misters, I welcome you to San Miguel de Los Bancos. We are very proud to have you here. Let me introduce myself; my name is Pablo Mendoza, long-time resident and citizen of San Miguel de Los Bancos." He was indeed an old fellow, spindly but spry. Gray whiskers grizzled his chin and a broad smile supported an equally broad nose. His eyes peeked out below the rim of a white straw hat that matched his shirt and light trousers.

"Gentlemen," he said, "I have a request, or I should say, we the people of Los Bancos have a request. We are in a terrible state and in desperate need of a bridge on my land across the rushing Río Blanco. The bridge is not for us so much as it is for our children, who must cross the bridge every day to attend the beautiful school we now have in our town. Right now they use nothing but a cable and stick affair. It is very dangerous. They should have a better bridge."

Looming over the man, Bob answered in his most pompous manner, "Well sir, we're from the Peace Corps, and don't really know much about bridges, but we thank you for your request."

Reassured, Pablo Mendoza shook our hands saying, "Thank you, Señores. You're very kind. I know you'll do good things. Thank you for listening to me." Bowing slightly he returned to his store front. We continued to the school.

Huge sheets, reflecting the tropical sun, had been draped across the soccer field at the back of the school. An aging woman in a heavy black dress, no doubt the helper Oswaldo had spoken of, clung to sheet corners and swung them in an effort to create the proper signal. Pupils chased all about, helping and hindering with the arrangement of the sheets.

Acción Cívica took an air of command. First they drove their truck onto the field to have the fuel close to the helicopter and then ran it back out in fear it would be in the way. They checked their watches, conferred and scoured the billowy blue sky for signs of an approaching craft.

At the appointed hour, a speck appeared out of the east and circled the town. All residents collected in a deep swathe around the jungle clearing and tittered as the bright orange bird of the Ecuadorian Air Force made its final descent. With the whir of the wind and whipping of blades, people scurried around corners and dove for cover intimidated by the alighting force.

Once the helicopter was down and the blade slowed, the crowd pressed forward for a closer inspection. Three bodies moved inside the spherical cockpit flipping switches and releasing themselves from their safety belts. With a flourish they threw open the side door and disembarked, resembling the crew of *Star Trek* with elegant, bright-orange scarves wrapped around their necks and tucked into the top of slick silk uniform.

Great ceremony was made of protocol and introductions of the arriving heroes. Bob and I, who had been shuttled to the front, chatted with them in English which they had learned at their pilot training in Arizona.

Our little nucleus turned into a procession, and then a parade. We marched up and down the one street in Los Bancos, giving ourselves a small tour while the townspeople ran ahead and behind and stood in their doors to get a glimpse of the assorted strangers who had assembled in their town on this sunny, tropical day. The parade ended at an open-air restaurant set with long tables where we feasted and were feted and served with the utmost hospitality.

Soon we walked back to the helicopter to continue our tour of the jungle zone we had come to develop and integrate into the rest of the Western World. A crowd escorted us back and curious onlookers pressed forward to load us on board. As we rose into the sky a scene of diving bodies and fleeing dogs bade us farewell.

Swooping into the air, then dropping into the deep canyon of the Río Blanco, our pilot gave us an exhilarating exhibition of the dynamics of jungle topography and the abilities of his machine. Down we floated through the canyon's features; up we soared high over cliffs and across thick, uninhabited jungle. As we moved towards the wide Guayllabamba River, only an occasional clearing with human habitation appeared,

In the back of Acción Cívica's brown Chevy pickup with Sargento Jerez.

including one that Oswaldo Berni pointed out as Pachijal. Swinging back south, we searched out the road and followed it west where bright yellow machines battled their way further into the jungle's secretive soul. Twirling around, we moved back up the road to another clearing of many buildings, more gathering crowds and billowing sheets.

The settlement at Kilometer One Sixteen: We didn't know them; they didn't know us. We were about to land.

Twice
Flattened

A GROWING NUMBER of privately owned vehicles crowding the streets was a logical outcome of upper-class North Quito assimilating a lifestyle of American consumerism. Instead of using the buses — which functioned perfectly well — the wealthy now rode in their own cars. In time this created another problem for this age-old city — traffic congestion. The Ecuadorian solution (likely due to American urban planners loaned to the Ecuadorian government) was the same one as the United States came up with in the 1950's: freeways.

When I arrived in these mountains, there were three freeways in and around Quito, but thanks to loans from the Inter-American Development Bank, this situation was changing rapidly. One of the three freeways began at the southern end of Quito's Mariscal Sucre International Airport's major runway and zoomed through the newly created sprawl of North Quito until it narrowed to two lanes and entered general chaos as it approached Avenida Colón.

We lived near this congestion after fleeing the suburbs of North Quito. Emil, Lorenzo and I finally decided that we had not traveled 6,000 miles to live in an American ghetto. So Emil went back on the prowl and found a second-story flat one block from where the freeway coming from the airport ended. Our new home was a convenient one: far enough up a side street to avoid the noise of this traffic jumble and luckily out of the path of destruction of the impending road expansion that was designed to extend the freeway toward downtown Quito. Demolition was proceeding from the north and the south and the stretch of old buildings where only two rows of traffic could squeeze through, were coming closer by the day to their demise.

Our favorite spot along this imperiled stretch was El Pájaro Loco (The Crazy Bird) a traditional Ecuadorian restaurant with attractively low prices. El Pájaro Loco's entire twenty foot width opened onto the street where a woman sat in a cashier's stand at one side and tables stretched along the opening to the street. Wooden and rickety, set in long rows, the tables were covered with plastic cloths. Fifteen feet in from the street, halfway to the back wall of the restaurant, a waitress bided her time in another wood and glass enclosure. Across from her, against the wall, a juke box blasted a rollicking *cumbia* beat. The rear was unlit and a door led through the back wall to other rooms which belched bursts of laughter followed by strings of curses.

We always sat at a street-side table where they served us *churrascos*, the best deal in town. For fifteen *sucres* El Pájaro Loco offered these gastronomic delights on an elliptical platter heaped with fried potatoes and a chunk of meat topped with a couple of fried, still runny-yoked eggs. Fresh lettuce, beets, onions and avocados decorated the sides.

From our table we could survey the buildings —including El Pájaro Loco — that were marked for destruction. Beside us rose El Teatro Colón, one of the city's oldest movie houses. A fine thick adobe structure, its roof curved fifty feet above the ground and sweeping adornments decorated the upper reaches of its pale yellow face. Below, small arches led theater goers into interior elegance, soon to fall before the relentless swing of the wrecking ball.

On the opposite side of this two-lane bottleneck, another series of buildings awaited a similar fate. Across from El Teatro Colón, heavy adobe walls of typical pastel yellow enclosed a small paint shop just large enough for two people. One of the occupants was the old, hobbled proprietor who leaned against a wooden counter to deal with the one customer who could enter from the street. Behind him, stacked on narrow shelves from the plank floor to the plaster roof were containers of odd and assorted lacquers, enamels, bases and varnishes. Sixteen pints of yellow sat next to a quart of purple set on top of a gallon of clear finish. Dust clung to the supplies he had been overzealous in procuring. To requests for a certain variety he often shook his haggard head and rocking his wearied hand in a circular motion replied, *"No hay."* (The typical refrain for a country eternally beset by shortages, *no hay* — pronounced no eye — means that there isn't any.) He stocked what he could, customers took what he had.

Down a few doors — private entrances to the interior — a burly man ran a *tienda*, a corner store, an Ecuadorian custom that puts eggs, milk, small supplies of dried goods, produce, stationery, tape and sundry other items within steps of the entire country's front door. Within the tienda there was more area than in the paint shop, but the customer still had no space, myriad boxes and bottles taking up the floor. One of these stores could be found every few blocks. There was another around the corner, below our apartment and another beyond it. They were functional community hubs, distributing newspapers, providing telephone service, refrigeration, gossip and other community services. Along with the community it served, this *tienda* was destined to be plowed under by the forthcoming freeway and the American, European and Japanese cars that would drive over its surface.

Across an alley, large blue wooden folding doors opened into an extensive hardware facility operated by several generations of one family. They advised and provided local residents all the tools and supplies needed to repair ailing items within their aging homes. They talked, dickered, bartered and laughed with the people they had been doing business with for years.

A small dead-end street separated the next cluster of low, one-story adobe buildings. These were a mystery to me and I had an opportunity to enter only a few of them before their demolition. Two rooms opened onto the streets from this block-square labyrinth of rooms and residences. One was a small snack shop where a slender, aging gentleman sold ice cream to us on hot Quito mornings. The other was around the corner on the street leading to our second-story flat. As this street sloped up, the floor of the buiding fell below the street level, bringing the building's red tile roof even with my head. Raw, brown, mud-covered walls faced the street. Dry, earthen goo held sun-baked bricks in place. Heavy wool blankets, dancing in cross breezes, hung over the openings to the interior.

From the raised road we could peer into the barren home of a crinkled old woman and the many small children she cared for. Her old, dark-blue woven flap hung over her doorway and was frequently tied back, making her abode a scene of the street and the street part of her home. Her one room resembled the quarters of a family living far out in the hills with a dirt floor and no electricity. Only the tiles on the roof separated her family from harsh mountain rains and nothing stopped bitter cold from sweeping through cracks and past the blanket to violate the room. Rain leaks were the only running water that entered and heat came from either an open fire or her one-burner stove. Tarnishing black soot covered the walls and the smoke escaped where it could.

In the early morning hours she sat near the door sharing her wrinkled visage with each passerby. Her face was a dark, weathered brown. Short and wide, creases of age crossed it from all sides. In the fashion of the campesinas, her graying black hair wound in long braids down her back and full skirts flared from her bulging middle. All about bounded the children of her charge, small girls, three, maybe five years old; from what origins I have no idea. Most likely they were grandchildren, trusted to the care of the old mother.

Before her on the curb in these bright hours after dawn, sat an old metal iron, its hollow insides filled with hot glowing coals. It was a tool of her daily struggle for the food and clothing necessary to keep her brood living. Working totally by hand, she repaired damaged shoes.

Lorenzo once had her install a heel on his boot. She charged him almost nothing and we inspected her work upon its completion. With dexterous fingers and a sharp knife she had molded a piece of rubber to fit over the worn heel. The bottom was flattened in a similar manner for a comfortable step. Tiny nails, only slightly larger than a pin, had been driven through the rubber into the old sole.

Her clientele was small, her labor slow. How she ever generated enough income to keep her family going I could not imagine.

Hidden within the stolid mud walls that encircled this doomed block existed dozens of families under similar conditions. How many, I could not say. I only caught glimpses of their lifestyles through doors inadvertently left ajar. Within, I observed a series of single-room habitations closely packed about a common patio. One faucet served as a communal watering hole and no sanitary facilities were available. Each room, ten by twenty, held as many as five people, and there may have been fifty rooms in this block of dark squalor. Perhaps one hundred and fifty people called it the only home they had. They were one step ahead of the people sleeping on the Plaza de Santo Domingo, but not for long.

We had no idea how many people lived in this "casbah" until we were sitting at El Pájaro Loco, chewing down *churrascos* on the day that monstrous machines began tearing it all down. Then the people streamed out like ants under attack with no control over their fate. Tension mounted at the scene as more and more people began milling on the street, mixing with the traffic and chaos already existing along that short stretch of roadway.

We watched as a couple of guys in thickly-knit blue sweaters, now probably wearing all the clothes they owned, picked up some pieces of fallen debris and flung them at the steel machines. It was an idea whose popularity gained momentum and soon there was a small army flinging stones at the demolition crew.

Alarmed, the policeman at the corner came waving his arms but was unable to do a thing against the torrent of stones and dust that was now flying through the air. Buses halted, traffic came to a stop and then the troops showed up. In a country run by a military general, these soldiers carried semi-automatic rifles and were not worried about the repercussions of their use. Gulping down our *churrascos*, we scattered along with the now homeless and ragged "troublemakers."

With their homes destroyed, I have no idea what happened to the former residents of this block. The ice cream man was gone and the old lady too; so were her kids and her repairing of shoes. They were run off by an influx of cars and honking horns that descended on this city in consumptive droves.

After the destruction of the buildings along the route, the pace of the project slowed to that of manual labor and blocked traffic. Only southbound private vehicular traffic was allowed to pass through the construction area. Everything else was sent scattering through narrow side streets. In an ironic twist of revealing decision-making, while private autos used the main road, buses that had historically used this route were now forced onto a labyrinth of side streets. All northbound traffic suffered a similar fate, sending confusion and noise into previously tranquil neighborhoods.

Eventually a long, deep trench and mounds of earth stretched along the future freeway. During the workday there was always a bustle of workers surrounding this trench.

Sometimes, setting forth on early morning activities, I passed by this excavation and stopped to reflect on the scene. All along the trench, and interspersed among the piles of dirt and construction materials, were dozens of workers. These were not the hard-hat, well-paid, union laborers seen in the States, but rather a collection of *campesinos* hired at minimal wages to perform the backbreaking work that animals and machines do in other parts of the world. Women, often carrying babies on their backs, worked next to men hauling heavy loads of materials from one spot to another.

Once as I was strolling along with Emilio we stopped to gaze at the scene before us. Watching a stooped woman wheel a load of dirt, I shook my head and muttered a question about how much these people got paid. Patting me on the back Emil nodded, "Oh, Jimbo, old boy. You wouldn't want to work for the wages these guys make. I think we're looking at about thirty-five *sucres* a day, if these guys are lucky, and they don't look too lucky to me."

"So, that's about a dollar sixty a day, huh? That ain't much money."

"Yep," said Emil. "Well, Mr. Economista, how come you figure that we get about five times that much and, even though I hate to admit it, we don't really have to do anything?"

"That, my boy, is a good question, and perhaps the crux of the matter. I think the truth is that we won the lottery. You and I were born in the

States; these people were born in Ecuador. They're building a road so that the rich folk can drive their Detroit-built cars down the freeway. Rich Ecuadorians send their profits to Detroit to buy cars. Detroit pays taxes to the government and the government pays us. So in a rather perverse manner, these workers are subsidizing our income. At the same time, of course, it's draining their economy of funds that could be used to pay them better wages. So what do you think of my explanation?"

"Well, it doesn't make one feel like the champion of the world," Emil pondered, looking up at the sky. Then with a sly smile he looked back at me and said, "But I do suppose, old boy, that if anybody is going to win the lottery, it might as well be your friend and mine, Emil J. Peterson."

"Yeah, but look, Emil," I answered, "these folks are double losers with this project. Not only did they have their homes demolished across the way there and now have to sleep on the street, but they are forced to work at starvation wages on a project that only promises to make their plight worse."

The Greatest Show in the Jungle

Presidents, fiestas, races
and all
Make packages of fun
that always enthrall.
Jungle residents lurch
and reel through their paces
To hear long-winded speeches
and behold our smiling white faces.

EVERYBODY LOVES A PARTY and Ecuadorians are no exception. Acción Cívica didn't do much, but they did throw a big fiesta. "Development Days" in Los Bancos wallowed in cane alcohol and flashed through gambling tournaments. People packed the schoolhouse, rocking and rolling to a thriving *cumbia* beat produced by five jivers and their collected instruments. It refused to stop. It was going at 2:30 AM as we climbed rickety stairs to blanket-on-board beds above the fly-bitten Salon de Puerto Quito. It was going a couple of hours hours later when a horde of tired drunks burst through our door to claim our beds. It was going at sunrise as I stumbled to the street to wash my face, where I was met by a bottle-swinging local and his god-awful *trago*.

Lanky, sweaty and slightly hunched, he spotted me at the faucet. "Hey mister, *salud, salud,*" and with a nod took two shots of his fiery potion. "Ya, mister, drink it, *salud,*" and with a long arc, swept the bottle in my direction.

"No, no, no thanks, not now," I assured him, my head still reeling from the home-made cane alcohol I had consumed the night before.

"Sure mister, drink up, *salud.*"

"No, no thanks."

Disbelieving my protestations, he pressed on, "*Salud,* mister, drink."

I faced the inevitable; it scorched as it went down. A great beginning — a little like never ending yesterday.

This was the day of the race. In an effort to maximize publicity for the Pilot Program of Development in the Northwest of Pichincha Province under the auspices of Acción Cívica of the Armed Forces of the Nationalist and Revolutionary Government, Oswaldo Berni hatched a truly incredible scheme: a car race from Quito along tight roads and perilous cliffs to Los Bancos. I laughed when someone first mentioned racing this route and cried when I realized they were serious. I was paralyzed with fear just driving it carefully. Racing it was certain suicide, true machismo. Oswaldo Berni, of course, wasn't driving, he was just promoting.

Expectation captivated Los Bancos. People waited all day, boozed a lot, sunned a lot, partied a lot. Few witnessed the finish of the race. I was lingering over one of the race cars when the next surprise literally descended upon us.

I first noticed the whup, whup, whup of big blades beating the air. Everyone looked up, yelled, screamed and started running. A speck out of the East became a helicopter as it circled the town and alighted in the school yard. I trudged after the crowd. Whispers, *"El Presidente, El Presidente, ya viene El Presidente."*

So it was. Through the glass doors came the bulging torso of Generalísimo Guillermo Rodríguez Lara, *El Presidente de la República.* The mass of ragged campesinos, sun-glassed military, city bureaucrats, drunken card players, race drivers and the President paused by the turbo-propped chopper before moving in my direction. Approaching, the crowd opened like a blooming flower revealing General Rodríguez Lara strolling directly toward me.

A short man, he was informally dressed in tan pants and a light-yellow shirt open at the neck. Round and solid, his body deserved the endearment "Bombito" (water balloon) which had been conferred upon him by his countrymen. His complexion indicated that he came from a mixed-blood, mestizo family. Broad glasses rested on pudgy cheeks and a short mustache decorated his upper lip. An expansive, felt cowboy hat covered a balding dome and a fat ring wrapped around his right middle finger. On his belt he carried a small revolver. Behind him strode an ominous military guard — lurking eyes behind obscure sun glasses kept the crowd on edge.

Only feet away, the President eyed me. "Weho, woh har you?"

I was stunned. I sensed that he was speaking to me, but I didn't understand a word he said, didn't even know what language he was speaking.

"Weho, wouh har you?" He said it again. He was speaking English, something he had learned in high school years before. Flustered, I responded in Spanish, wishing to avoid a conversation in English I couldn't understand. But he persisted, proving to the crowd that he could handle himself internationally as well as locally.

I was speechless and finally mumbled something back in Spanish. Perhaps sensing my unease, he nodded and moved on. Saying little, he proudly marched up the street and then back down, the crowd surrounding him on all sides. He smiled a few times, got in a few pictures, returned to his helicopter and was off.

The fiesta, the President, the race were part of a show, a much bigger show aimed at convincing people that something was happening in a sea of stagnation. Bob and I were part of the show. Oswaldo toured us around, but we said very little. At community meetings he propped us up on stage though we contributed nothing. At one point we protested.

"Here, come up on the stage," Oswaldo encouraged us before a meeting at the Kilometer One Sixteen schoolhouse. "These chairs are for you."

"No, no thanks, we'll just stay down here," we assured him.

"Oh, come on up. It's better if you're up here," he insisted.

"No," we said, "we don't have anything to contribute."

"Sure you do; people feel better about the program if they see a couple of Americans up here." And so it was, our smiling faces shone at all ends of the zone.

Additional helicopter rides became an important element in this circus. Not only did they tweak the interest of the residents, they also attracted the bureaucrats from the city. Acción Cívica had a big meeting in Los Bancos of representatives from all the government ministries. Their bait — free helicopter rides — brought dozens of officials many twisting miles to Los Bancos. It also brought the press and television. They touted El Plan Piloto de Desarrollo en el Noroccidente de Pichincha as a great effort by the administration to develop and change Ecuador and the world.

Acción Cívica eventually established a council of local residents to give opinions on this project and deal with the government bureaucracies. In turn, a plan demanding eighteen major projects was presented by the local committee to Acción Cívica. Oswaldo Berni subsequently confided to me with a shake of the head, "Those are the wrong people to have on that committee; we're going to have to dissolve them and start a new one."

Acción Cívica did supervise the construction of a community house and barracks for the half dozen soldiers they stationed in the area. In the entire time I was there, I never saw the soldiers do anything except pose for a picture working with civilians.

As for the community house, the largest structure in the area, I saw it used only once as a community center. That was when the President came back to dedicate it with his military-political entourage in tow.

On a bright sunny day, the heat soaking moisture from the soggy jungle floor, his counselors and cabinet members filled a specially constructed reviewing stand at the Casa Comunal. Forest inhabitants trudged miles to see the man who ruled the countryside and his band of advisors.

Officials, one by one, stepped to the microphone with long, glowing speeches about the virtues of the government and the Pilot Program and the future of the "zone." It was truly a show.

El Presidente, however, topped them all. Dressed in simple green fatigues of the working military, stepping to the podium amidst cheers, he waited for the crowd to quiet. Slowly he began his oratory. Talking expansively of the world and his administration, he spoke of the right of people to land, though he didn't mention that the wealthy had rights to the cleared and accessible land and the poor to the untamed, inaccessible, unwanted land.

He spoke of how his coming and the coming of the whole world economy was good, for while he recognized that there were evil elements in the international marketplace, He, *El Presidente de la República*, could slay those devils and preserve the benefits of international capitalism for the average Ecuadorian. He spoke of OPEC and the Andean Pact, local monopolies to confront multinational monopolies. He did not mention that a worker is a worker, no matter who his employer, and that all these people were destined to work less for themselves and more for someone else.

Little matter what he didn't say: what he did say was captivating. Not only what he said, but what he did. An hour after beginning, he flailed his arms in bombastic histrionics. After another hour he was shimmying and shaking and shouting at the top of his voice. I had no idea where he got his endurance. Personally I got tired just listening and went inside to nibble at the waiting feast. By the time he was finished, most of the people who could were inside nibbling.

El Presidente entered full of enthusiasm. He chatted from group to group. We met at the end of the long banquet table where he remembered me and chatted in Spanish about long hair, snow and the United States. Then he was off into another conversation.

After lunch he moved with gusto up the road toward the mountains, through the towns of Andoas, Kilometer One-O-One, Los Bancos, Mindo and beyond. At least fifty cars loaded with advisors and courtiers followed him. At each spot, crowds gathered and he gave similar speeches. His emphasis didn't change: land for the people, Ecuador for the Ecuadorians, and struggles against the multinational corporate invaders. They were all popular themes.

Unfortunately, the aristocrats, the wealthy, the powerful, the ones to whom El Presidente owed his compromised office, did not consider them popular themes. They counseled El Bombito to limit his actions if not his words. Heeding sage advice Guillermo Rodríguez Lara guaranteed that the show went on, and that the programs didn't. Unlike other nations (Chile, Cuba, Vietnam), Ecuador never challenged the basic tenets of private property and little changed. Few peasants got the land they needed and few multinational corporations were ever confronted. However, the show did go on — down the road, over and over and over again.

Rock Spirits
in the
Automobile Graveyard

GRATING AND FRICTION between Ecuadorian and American life styles racked my soul as the curdling of one society refused to mix with the bubbling values of the other. I sought refuge to create a balance of my own but only tumbled further into the cultural brew.

Across the valley and over low hills that drop into the old town of Guapolo, I met the Vivar family and found sanctuary within their automobile junkyard. When Don Celso Vivar first gave me a tour, my future home appeared to be a gloomy cellar filled with rats and tarantulas. Windows were broken and dirty, doors hung off their hinges and mounds of rusted auto parts cluttered every corner. It did have a spacious verandah, though, along with a view of the colonial Guapolo Monastery, lush rolling hills, and Tumbaco Valley spreading east to 20,000-foot snow-capped peaks of the eastern range of the Andes Mountains. Its rooms were spacious but completely uninhabitable. I said I would think about it. Don Celso said I would have to talk to his wife.

I met her on my way out the wooden gates which separated the junk-yard from the street. She was shorter and plumper than her old mate, wrapped in shawls, sweaters and heavy woolen skirts. Stringy, light-gray hair hung over her aged bronzed head and calculating eyes flicked behind thick-rimmed glasses. She pursed her lips when talking, allowing a smile only when it suited her needs.

Don Celso pointed her out as he fled into his back-room office and she eyed me warily as I greeted her, *"¿Señora Vivar?"*

She responded with a suspicious, "Good day, Señor Mister, and what may I call you?"

"Señor Tarbell, it is," I said taking her hand in the traditional Ecuadorian greeting.

"Tarbell, that's a funny one," she said dropping my hand. "Don't you have another?"

Taken off guard, I pondered for a minute. "Another name?" I paused, "Some people call me Diego."

"Diego?," she mumbled softly, "Diego, Diego." Then with a bright twist she said, "Then Diego it is. What can I do for you Señor Diego?"

"I wondered if you had a small place I could rent to live in."

With a broad smile coming to her face she said, "So, my husband, Don Celso, showed you this place back here. What do you think of it?"

Staring in amazement I said, "I need a place I can live in."

"You can live there," she responded indignantly.

"It's a mess."

"I'll fix it up."

"What'll you do, tear it down?"

Shaking her wrinkled head she said, "No, no, no. I'll put a toilet and a shower in one room and a sink for a kitchen in the one next to it. Don't worry. I'll fix it all up."

"Along with the crumbling walls," I asked in disbelief, "and broken windows and collapsing doors?"

"Sí, sí, Diego, we'll fix it all up," she shook her head vigorously, disgusted with my doubts.

"How soon will it be done?"

"When do you want it?"

"Next month."

"It'll be done. You can pay fifteen hundred *sucres*?"

"To repair your shack?"

"To rent it."

"Too high, I'll go a thousand."

She smiled, "Bueno, Señor Diego, it's a deal." We shook.

Two months and several advance rental payments later —to finance her reconstruction project — her workers had renovated the interior. Outside, the verandah had been cleared of littered mechanical paraphernalia and a short wall had been constructed to separate my quarters from the happenings in Don Celso's automobile graveyard. Waist-high and five feet long — leaving space to enter from the junkyard onto the front patio of my transformed home — this wall divided the Latin life of the junkyard and the North American atmosphere brewing in my new house.

The lively atmosphere on the Ecuadorian side was maintained by a constant flow of personalities. Four of these characters were perennially on the scene: Don Celso, master of the junkyard; Virginia, his wife, my landlady; Andrés, a stocky mechanic; and Rene, their other, younger mechanic.

Andrés and Rene worked more as demolition experts than as mechanics, pulling old, maimed autos apart and putting them together in entirely new forms.

Andrés, the older of the two, once told me that he had shown up at this hillside lot six days a week for twenty-two years. He was a short, solid fellow of strong Andean features, with skin showing a smooth brown where it was not covered by his drab olive clothes. His thick neck supported a hard-cornered head which featured a broad nose, slightly jowled cheeks, a protruding chin, deep inset eyes and ears flattened far back on the side of his head. He invariably wore a battered broad-brimmed hat that matched his drab apparel and hid a lush flow of grease-black hair which he combed from the top of his high forehead back over the rim of his skull.

True to his Andean heritage, Andrés had been raised in a rural setting across the valley on the slopes of Mount Cayambe. He often told me stories and made observations that pointed out how the perceptions of his indigenous upbringing varied from my viewpoint nurtured in American suburbia.

Andrés always hailed me as I entered or exited through the junkyard and one day as I entered I could tell that he was particularly agitated.

"Don Diego," he waved, "Don Diego, how are you today?"

Walking over to shake his hand I responded, "Fine, and yourself?"

Hesitatingly he said, "I'm all right." Then after a short pause he continued, "Say, Diego, could I ask you a question?"

"Sure."

"We had a strange thing happen."

"What was that?"

"Well, the other day my neighbors and I . . . You know where I live, Don Diego, way over on the other side of the valley on the side of Mount Pichincha?"

"Uh huh."

"We went with the *ingeniero* (engineer) way back above our *ba-rrio*. We went way up in the hills, on the sides of the peaks of Mount Pichincha looking for water. We went a long way from anyone's house. We were walking along a very narrow and winding path, like the ones they have up there. On one side the ground fell off very steeply, straight down for a long ways. On our other side the mountain rose very high. We were walking along a particularly narrow part of the path when we heard a great crash. It was a big crash that went kawhomp!"

Circling his arms in the air, the memory of the noise ignited lights in his eyes. "When we heard it, we turned and ran. Then we heard another noise, a rumbling from above and stopped to see what was happening. A big boulder, huge, gigantic, the size of your house came bounding down the hill and smashed right on the path where we had been standing.

"Why, if we hadn't run, Diego, we would have been crushed. If that noise hadn't warned us, we would have been killed. It saved our lives!

"What do you think made that noise, Diego? What could have warned us like that?"

"I imagine," I replied in my best western scientific mode, perplexed that he would have such a question, "that it was the rock rolling down the hillside."

"No, Diego," he shook his head, "it wasn't the same noise. It was a sharper sound like thunder, but it was a clear day. What do you think made

"It was a big crash that went Kawhomp!"

Rock Spirits in the Automobile Graveyard

that noise? I think it was the Spirit of the mountain itself. The Spirit of Mount Pichincha that didn't want us back there. It warned us and then threw that rock at us. What do you think of that?"

Stunned by the sincerity of his analysis I paused before again asking, "Are you sure it wasn't just the rock crashing down?"

"No, it was different, Diego. We all heard it. It was the Spirit of the mountain. When we saw that rock come down we ran back home. That Spirit doesn't want us back there. What do you think of that? The Spirit of Mount Pichincha!"

Mountain spirits throwing rocks? I shook my head, "I don't know, I do not know."

Meanwhile on my side of the short wall, a different sort of rock spirit blossomed under the equatorial sun and our carefree existence raised as much wonderment on the junkyard side of the wall as their stories raised on mine.

Red curtains on my warped windows blocked the curious peerings of my landlady and hid an interior of huge pillow couches and a musical system that blared the raucus tunes of Mick Jagger and Pink Floyd far over the valley below. Why red curtains? It was the decision of the installer, an old girlfriend from the states who flew in to share my gyrating life and was gone in a month, blown away by the contradictions and craziness of my Ecuadorian existence.

Such visits from single women were something to which Virginia hadn't been exposed and that she had not expected. They didn't set well in her mind. Neither did rock music or light which glowed through the red curtains late into the night.

Music attracted merriment and many visitors. Friends from the countryside, into the city briefly, rapped on my door in search of a bed and a refuge where they could privately practice the American lifestyle they had left in the States. Nothing was unusual about a bevy of folks strewn across the floor, over the pillows and inside beds. Melodious rock-and-roll floated through the night and reappeared with the rising sun.

Mornings were spectacular from my perch. The sun climbed out of the Amazon to shine over the blackened eastern ridge of the towering mountains. Instantaneously, clouds collected in the valley below reflected dazzling light from their billowing tops and the sun brightly illuminated lush, green hillsides that plummeted into the lingering fog.

It was a vision of rebirth and joy that my awakening crowd celebrated with the opening of windows, pumping of tunes and consumption of banana pancakes on the sun-baked veranda. There we lingered and lounged, men, women, boys and girls in all stages of dress. Hair to our knees, music surging from within, gay laughter exploding from our souls to our smiling faces. Unfortunately, these rituals weren't always so private.

From behind the junkyard corner, wrapped in a thick knit sweater and heavy black skirt, taking up a position opposite us at the end of the short dividing wall, was Virginia. She made a pretense of directing her attention toward activities in the junkyard, but guarded, carefully placed glances took in the scene unfolding on my front porch.

She didn't understand; she couldn't understand. She had never seen anything like it before. Long-haired men, skimpily-clad women, rollicking beats, scrumptious meals. And it was all taking place before her morning newspaper was delivered. She did not like it. She maintained her reticence over my strange lifestyle for eight months until finally, late one Saturday night, she exploded.

Earlier on that particular day, while waiting for some American neighbors to return, an acquaintance used my back room to do some yoga, probably in her underwear, if that, and undoubtedly my landlady took the whole scene in through some inadvertently open curtain. The acquaintance was gone by the time night fell and I was left to a rare peaceful evening in the silence of my home. About eight my buzzer rang and the gate opened to admit Patrick Doherty, in the city from Lago San Pablo. I welcomed his visit and we celebrated with customary cheer. Music flowed and we sat back to chatting and a long game of chess.

Hours passed and we were contemplating sleep when the buzzer rang again. With a mystified nod I stuck my head out the bedroom window to investigate who had pushed my buzzer so late at night. As I leaned out and stared up the street, I made out the faint image of Señora Vivar in a waist-length robe and a long, thick nightgown covering her legs.

"Hola, Señora Vivar. What's happening? What can I do for you?" I shouted through the dark of the night.

I could see her shaking as she began screaming, "Diego, what do you do? What's going on in there?"

"What do you mean?," I puzzled. "Nothing is wrong here."

"What do you do inside that house?," her shrill, angry cry blasted the night. "The gate is open and there are cars and people coming and going. Something bad is going on in there. I know it."

"What!" I replied in shocked astonishment. "That's crazy! There is nothing going on inside here."

By now she was directly below my window, carrying on at the top of her squeaky voice, waving her arms and throwing her index finger accusingly in my direction. "I am a woman of high standards, Diego, and I won't have your evil life being carried on in my house."

My mind whizzed for the cause of her accusation. "What are you talking about?" I shouted back, "What do you mean?"

"What do you do Diego? Run a *salón*? . . . with women. You gamble at your games and you blare your terrible music. Tell me what all those mattresses are for. I know what they are for. You run a salon Diego. I know it, and I won't have it in my house!"

Amazed at her assumptions and aghast at the eviction she was working up to I protested, "You're crazy. There's just one friend here. Come in right now and I'll show you nothing unusual is happening."

"No Diego," she sadly shook her head, "now is the time for decent people to be in bed."

Grasping for a thread of comprehension that would bridge the gap between our conflicting cultures, I insisted, "You don't understand. I use these pillows for chairs. I don't run a *salón*. I don't gamble at any games. We come from different cultures, that's all. It's a misunderstanding. Where I come from everything I do is normal."

"You're doing evil things, Diego. I don't know what they are, but I know you are doing evil things and I don't like it." With that she waddled back to her door, shaking her head in anger and disgust.

Sleeping little that night, I rose to confer with Don Celso as he wandered through the junkyard feeding his chickens at sunrise.

"Did you talk with Virginia last night?" I asked him.

In a supremely calm manner he walked amongst the chickens and replied. "I did, Diego. She thinks you're running a *salón*."

"With girls?"

"That's right. That's what she says. She says she sees carloads of people coming here. Personally, I don't believe a word she says. Old Virginia, she has visions, you know. She sees things. I know your friends. They're all good people."

"That's nice of you to say . . ." I paused with relief. "She upset me. Could you put in a good word for me and maybe bring her over to show her everything is all right?"

Smiling and placing his massive, aged hand on my back he reassured me, "Sure, Diego, I'll do that."

Several hours later he brought Virginia over for a tour that somewhat appeased her mind. She still seemed convinced there was evil in my life, but she did not kick me out. My life, however, continued as before, in a manner most mystifying and irritating to her.

Process to
Processed

*I*N GUAPOLO living like most Ecuadorians, without refrigeration, I bought food in the traditional markets where the breadth of Ecuadorian culture was always on display. This contrasted greatly with my experience in the suburbs of North Quito where we shopped at Supermercado La Favorita in the Comercio Central.

The dichotomy of these experiences was brought home to me one day when I went shopping at the neighborhood market in La Vicentina. It was a Thursday, the day for La Vicentina and, though selling started early, I wasn't in a hurry.

I walked from my house a little before ten, carrying on my arm a wicker *canasta*, a woven basket of thick dried reeds, just the right size to carry a babe newly born. I trudged up the hill to the end of the number thirteen bus line, where a blue *colectivo* sat with ten rows of seats and no one on board. The driver was reading his paper, ready to go and as soon as several passengers boarded he raced his engine and headed downtown.

I stayed on a dozen blocks or so, getting off by a large gurgling fountain at Avenida Madrid. Here I caught another *colectivo* coming out from downtown and headed to the left and La Vicentina. During these hours of the market the bus was stuffed full of people and, as was the custom in these cases, I boarded on the run. As it slowed for the corner, I ran to beat hell, leaping on the bottom step. The bus was so crowded, that was as far as I got. My feet on the step, my fingers grasping the handle, I hung out in the breeze, the *canasta* bobbing in the wind. A few blocks further on, as passengers departed, I was sucked through the door into the mass of bodies. Some people laughed, some shouted. It was a compact world of social interplay.

I remained inside past a circle and a plaza into the *barrio* where the market took place. Trees lined the streets of tightly packed two-story adobe houses decorated with grill work. At the end of the street and around a corner, the scene of the market, and all the colors it included, flourished into view. It lay before a meadow of lush, tufted grass, below a hillside of homes and the Vía Oriental. Delivery trucks from the countryside parked in the rear and in the open space between us spread the produce they brought.

Stepping from the bus I pondered which way to go. Besides the open field there was a permanent white building where people sold meat and dairy products in individual stalls. There nothing was wasted and all was put to use. Nausea rose in my soul as I plodded through the meat market. Thick oozing blood dropped into puddles from fresh hanging cows' heads, while flies and humans scrambled to claim the dead flesh as theirs. The stench suffocated my pores and the thud shook my mind as butchers axed the animals apart.

Outside, gentility returned and softness expanded in the slow padding feet of the old country women who came from the land where the food was produced. Their grins were bare-toothed as they chatted with friends and spun in their hands the wool for their clothes. A rhythm flowed in those slow moving hands as nimble, curved fingers twisted around a worn wood stick of some local tree, developing thereon a bulb of wool thread pulled from a sheered clump hidden deep in their clothes. They performed this intricate craft with nary a thought, providing warmth for themselves and their families from the teachings of time.

I gingerly entered this world of aged female vendors seeking the substance and basis that kept my life going. Before buying anything I inspected all items, sauntering through the dirt from one row to the next. The outer course of stalls was of the stand-up variety with a wide selection of vegetables piled as high as my head. On top sat the sales lady, wheeling and dealing and bargaining her goods. In the interior of the area there were no upright stands, just blankets on the ground stacked high with various goods. Tomatoes, carrots, squash, lettuce and other vegetables filled all the stalls along this first passage. Around the corner were artichokes and then wild herbs and teas. At the end was more produce in a confusion of stands.

In the next area vendors sold fruits of all types and toward the end of the row were flowers, vases and pots; then back to more fruit where my buying began.

After inspecting the whole field, I walked to a stand and softly felt a yellowing papaya. The seller, a middle-aged woman I had dealt with before, caught my activity in the corner of her eye and acknowledged my presence with a wave of her hand. She was busy at the moment with several other customers so I perused her selection and got in when I could.

Picking up a papaya and inspecting its surface I greeted her, "Good day, Madame, how much is this papaya going to cost me today?"

"Oh mister, that's good papaya, the best you can buy. I'll sell you those big ones for three *sucres* each."

"These papayas, they're not so big, but these oranges here, what do they cost?"

"Oranges are at five *sucres* a dozen, but here," grabbing a banana and waving it in my face, "you should buy these today; they are oh so delicious." Then changing focus she turned her attention to another customer, telling her, "Señora, buy these pineapples, they're juicy and fat . . ."

Meanwhile, I looked over her lot, dropping a dozen oranges in my *canasta*, then a couple of papayas. Next I grabbed a bunch of bananas to see if they were what she said. Her pricing seemed high, a typical ploy, and I calculated in my head what I should offer in return. I should definitely go low, almost to absurdity, then when we agreed, it would be an equitable deal.

"Say, Señora," I said, catching her attention, "I've got a dozen oranges and a couple of papayas and this bunch of bananas, I'll buy the whole lot for a price of nine *sucres*."

Her earth-black eyes thinned to a sliver as she considered if what I was saying was right. "That's an outrage mister, you couldn't be right. The oranges are at five, the papayas at three each and the bananas are two, so that's thirteen *sucres* to me."

"But Señora, these oranges are withered and tiny in size, and these bananas I could buy two hundred in the jungle for the price you want."

Brushing her hair back on her broad forehead she replied, "Mister, I am a poor woman, I work very hard, and I am giving you a very good deal. Look, I'll sell you this pineapple along with what you've got, charge you fifteen *sucres* and call it a deal.

Taking the pineapple in hand, I eyed her sly smile. "I don't want this pineapple, especially at six *sucres*. I'll pay you twelve for the whole lot, or ten for what I've got now."

"Mister, I must make some money. I'll sell what you've got in your basket at twelve-fifty and that's final."

"Señora, I'm making a quantity purchase. I'll pay you ten-fifty, but that's all I can do."

Horrified, she turned to another buyer. "Did you hear that? He says ten *sucres* is a big purchase. That's unbelievable." Shaking her head, she turned back to me. "I can't spend my day dickering with you. I'll sell you that fruit for twelve *sucres*, but that's it."

Shaking my head, I stubbornly replied, "I'll buy at eleven-fifty, and that's paying too much."

Eyeing me suspiciously she gave a few quick twists of her head and assented, "All right then, eleven-fifty it is, but give it to me quick. I have a lot more to sell."

Fishing in my pocket I pulled out various coins and handed her the agreed amount. As she counted it out a happy grin returned to her face, but then she grabbed the unbought pineapple and said, "Don't you want this? I'll only charge you four *sucres*."

"Four *sucres*!" I was aghast, "You were just going to charge me two."

"Four *sucres* is a good price. Look how juicy it is."

"Two-fifty, and that is all I'll pay."

Nope, four *sucres* is final," and she put it back.

"Okay, I'll pay three *sucres*."

"No, I'll only take four."

"Sorry, I can't do it," and I turned with my *canasta* to see the next vendor.

I was no more than three steps away when I heard, "Mister, mister!" As I turned she was waving the pineapple in hand. "You said you'd pay three *sucres*. All right, it's yours."

Walking back the few paces, I took the pineapple and placed it in my basket. Handing her the money I nodded my thanks, "*Gracias, Señora,* have a nice day." Oblivious to my salutation, she was already bargaining with somebody else.

Turning to assess the crowded market, I wandered along this back part absent-mindedly inspecting the other fruits available. Meandering along, purchases rolling about the bottom of my basket, I felt a slight tugging at my sleeve."

"Mister, mister, you want me to carry your *canasta* don't you?"

Bouncing around my feet were three young fellows no higher than my belt. They had no shoes and their light pants took the color of the earthen field. One wore a bulky knit sweater, larger than needed, and with so many holes the garment was useless. The other two wore long-sleeved cotton shirts, frayed at the cuffs that they pushed up their arms to reveal their small hands. They all had dark round faces and thick tousled manes.

"*Sí,* mister, I'll carry your *canasta* for you. *Sí,* mister."

Knowing that they wanted some payment for this service, I shook my head and said, "No, it's not necessary, I can carry it myself."

"But mister, you'll buy lots of food. It'll be very hard for you. We had better carry it for you."

"No, no problem," I insisted, "I've carried it lots. I'm a big fellow. I can do it easily."

"Ahhh, mister, please let us carry your *canasta.*"

Trying to ignore this onslaught, I persisted, "No, I can do it myself."

As I walked off, they tagged along behind. "Mister, mister . . ." But I maintained a straight face and continued on my way, their cries slowly blending with the din of the increasingly crowded market.

By this time I had reached the edge of the field and turned to go down the next row. Spread along the ground to the right were the herb and tea merchants, withered old women, dried and aged like the products they sold. I knelt down by an ancient one to look at her wares and said, "Good morning, how are you?"

Slightly startled, she welcomed me with a toothless grin. "Yes, my gringo, what could I ever do for you?" She sat with her legs crossed and covered by numerous long skirts. Her sweater was well worn and rimmed-hat quite tattered, but her eyes sparked with the thought that I could want something from her.

Picking up a long branch with dried flowers, I asked. "What would one ever use these flowers for?"

"Well, my friend, these are all teas very good for one's body. You can brew that one there if you have trouble breathing and are coughing a lot. This here," she indicated a pile of wide brown leaves, "is good for headaches, and this one for sore muscles."

"Are all of these plants to cure something in your body? It's quite a supply."

"Some are cures, and some are just spices, flavoring and such. Here is cinnamon and peppers and many more things."

"I'd like to have a little of that tea that's good for colds, and some cinnamon too."

She grabbed a handful of the dried flowers, wrapped them in old newspaper and dropped them in my *canasta*. She did the same with the cinnamon, meticulously wrapping it into a neat little package that wouldn't spill when it got jostled around.

"The *cedrón* tea is a *sucre* and the cinnamon fifty *centavos*."

I didn't argue a whit and paid her the equivalent of six cents for the two. "Thank you Señora, for the lesson and the herbs."

Stuffing the money deep into her garments, she replied with that same toothless grin, "You're welcome, my gringo, come back. I'll help you whenever I can."

Standing and stretching, I continued walking down the row and then stopped to ponder what I needed. I reached into my basket and pulled out a banana, mindlessly stripping off its thin yellow cover. I held it high over my head as I nudged through a small crowd of people and savored its sweet flavor while looking at the vegetable stands.

"Hey mister, where have you been?" A *campesina* across the way caught my attention. In previous weeks I had bought from her stand and I sauntered over to see what she had.

"Good day, Señora," I greeted her, "how have you been?"

Feigning hurt she replied, "Not so well, mister, I haven't seen you in weeks. Surely you haven't been buying from other women here."

Turning my eyes to the sky I assured her, "Oh no, Señora, I only buy from you."

"Good," her smile returned, "now, what would you like."

From her I bought tomatoes, lettuce, cucumbers, celery, onions and other vegetable treats. We had a gracious bargaining session and when that was over I decided I was through.

With my basket overflowing, weighing down my arm, I headed for the buses that were waiting to leave. Selecting the next to depart was a bit of a sport but when one began pulling out, I knew that was it.

Food baskets belonging to passengers were piled next to the driver and I slipped mine into a small space before paying the fare. More shoppers piled on as the bus slowly made its way down the first block. It then increased to normal speed as the market receded from view. Market goers disembarked, a couple each block. I got off, alone, at the end of Avenida Madrid by the gurgling fountain and as I waited for the number thirteen bus I contemplated how I used to go shopping at La Favorita in North Quito

In the mall no one sold their goods from blankets in the dust. Goods were displayed in concrete and glass cases. In the drug store all the products were locked up in little bottles and the only way to tell what they were for was to read the foreign instructions. The quantities were small and the prices were high.*

At the south end of the mall, swinging glass doors led to La Favorita, a supermarket in the North American style. Grabbing a rolling shopping cart, I'd swing around the end of the mechanical cash registers and start

---

* Abbot Laboratories, Dow Chemical, Merck, Sharp and Dhome, Park Davis Co., Phelps Dodge, Scherling Plough and Sterling Drugs, all US corporations, had set up production facilities in Ecuador in the past ten years in an attempt to expand their markets throughout the Andean region.

down the aisles to see what to buy. Along the east wall a metal case, polished and painted white, displayed pre-packaged vegetables in clear-plastic wrappers. Picking up tomatoes in their packaged enclosure to inspect their quality, I couldn't tell a thing. I couldn't smell them or feel them or see if they were rotten. I had little choice but to take what I got. Printed in stark little letters on a white stick-on label was "2 lbs, 3 oz, 5 *sucres*/lb, 11 *sucres*." It was more than I needed, but there was not much choice. All the packages were the same size, so I'd take one and drop it inside my cart.

Further on I loaded a bag of oranges and coming to the end, turned the corner for aisle number two. On either side metal shelves were stacked high with boxes of spices and teas. They all had names, but my Spanish wasn't advanced enough to know their English translations. They were all tightly sealed so I couldn't open them and look. I bought a few for four *sucres* each and went on my way. I'd continue down these colorless and sterile aisles adding packages, boxes and such.

I talked to no one and nobody spoke to me; musical notes emenated from a loud speaker system. Occasionally I encountered employees in uniform green garb, but they ignored me and continued mindlessly stamping or re-arranging boxes.

I collected substantial loads and, while waiting in line, tried without success to add up all the items in my cart. When my turn arrived I would load everything on the counter and the sixteen-year-old checker wouldn't even look up to say "hi." Also dressed in company green, she mumbled the prices as she punched the machine. Ninety-four *sucres* twenty *centavos*, I handed her a hundred and pocketed the change.

Lifting the plastic bag containing my food proved quite an effort. I grimaced as I thought of the trip home. On the way out the door a uniformed guard smiled good-bye. He was dressed in brown with wide patent leather sashes and on his hip wore a holstered revolver.

Outside the door, of course there were no buses to carry me home, so all I could do was hire a cab.

Bananas

Certain of learned ways

off we went bouncing

Devising great plans,

to the whole world announcing

That the Northwest of Pichincha

was available and calling

Or was somebody telling me,

it was readied for mauling?

COFFEE, BANANAS AND CACAO bobbed through my head as we jounced down the Quito-Los Bancos Road a year after my first whirlybird introduction. With Bob gone by way of marriage back to the States, I had graduated from the nauseating and chilly rear of the brown Chevy pickup and was now wedged between the rotund Oswaldo Berni and our equally large chauffeur, the dauntless Sargento Jerez.

Images of a grand economic study and plan for the Northwest of Pichincha Province danced through my brain. What resources existed in this tropical land? How could they be exploited? Where could they be sold? How could this area, its residents and products be incorporated into the great global marketplace?

Selling products in other parts of the world, I assumed, was the best idea: food to Quito, wood to Japan, but most obviously, the traditional crops of Ecuador — bananas, coffee and cacao — to the United States. Historically it was the way Ecuador had survived.* If ever this road was completed to the coast, it would be natural to use it to transport products of the "zone" to the coastal ports and from there to the rest of the world.

Lush, untouched jungle slipped past the window. Jerez swerved to miss a spot that had been ceded to a perilous ravine in the last rain storm. He drew my attention with a blow from his heavy elbow. I remained silent, still not confident of my Spanish and wary of the treacherous path we were careening down.

"*Zhimmy, Zhimmy*," Jerez bellowed, "why are you so quiet? How come you don't talk? Tell us a joke, sing us a song."

"I am thinking of important things," I reproached him, "and willing us safely down this road."

"Now, now, there's no need to worry. Old Sargento Jerez will take care of you. I know this road like *las tetas de mi madre*. Isn't that right Oswaldo?"

A half snoozing Oswaldo Berni, slouched against the door, didn't answer.

"Well," Jerez continued, "if you can't tell a joke or sing me a song, at least tell me these important things you're thinking about. You're not thinking about these jungle women are you?"

"Nope, not ladies. I'm putting some thoughts into an economic study I'm doing in the zone out here. I've got to figure out how to measure all the economic factors statistically and whether we can get things like bananas down to the coast for export."

"Ah, Sargento, bananas." At the sound of food Oswaldo roused himself and joined in the conversation. "That's one thing this place has. They have lots of good bananas, and cheap."

"Bananas, *plátanos*, the jewels of Ecuador," exuded the sergeant.

"Say, Sargento, we ought to go down and buy some," Oswaldo piped up. "We could go get the best ones, clear at the end of the road."

---

* A typical one-crop export economy: Ecuador produced large quantities of cacao for export at the turn of the century until West Africa and the East Indies began producing it. Then Ecuadorian plantations grew coffee until Brazil and Colombia took over the market. In the late 1940s blight struck the Central American banana crop and Ecuador became the world's top banana.

80

"Good idea, Oswaldo," added Jerez. "I bet we could buy a whole branch for three *sucres*."

"Three *sucres* for a whole branch!," exclaimed Oswaldo. "Ho, ho, that is a good price! Hey, *Zhamez*, you want to buy some bananas?"

"Oh, I don't know," I responded.

"Three *sucres* for a branch," persisted Oswaldo, "I bet that's a lot cheaper than in the United States."

"I imagine so," I said, slightly embarrassed and not wanting to become involved in their wheelings and dealings.

"Oh, Sargento," Oswaldo jumped in with enthusiasm, "you wouldn't believe it. When I was in Nueva York prices were incredibly expensive. Hey *Zhamez*, what's a banana cost in the United States?"

"A banana?" Taken aback I paused. "Oh I don't know, maybe ten cents for one banana."

"Ten cents!" Oswaldo exclaimed, "How much is that in *sucres*?"

"Ten cents is about," I stopped, "oh, about two and a half *sucres*."

"Two and a half *sucres* for one banana!" Oswaldo was amazed. "And we buy two hundred here for almost the same price. That's unbelievable. Oh Jerez, these Americans, they're smart. They come down here, buy bananas cheap from the poor sweating farmer and sell them for two hundred times the price back in their own country!"

"Hey, Zhimmy," the sergeant jested me, "are you sure you don't work for one of those big banana companies?"

"That's it, Sergeant," Oswaldo chimed. "Those are the ones. For years and years they've come down here and given money to government officials and big landowners to make sure there's low-priced labor to grow cheap bananas. There's one they call 'Yunay,' its real name is United something. They must make incredible amounts of money on our bananas. Oh, you Americans, you're not dumb."

"Hey Oswaldo," Sergeant Jerez broke in, "here comes Tandayapa. You want to stop and talk to the teacher?"

"*Sí, sí*, stop, stop."

Crossing a small bridge, we halted by the only three buildings in Tandayapa; intersection, rest stop and the beginning of what Acción Cívica considered their zone of influence. While Oswaldo trundled off to find the teacher and Sargento Jerez relieved himself, I bought an orange and some salted beans from an old man in a plank shack twelve feet long and six feet wide. Half the wall hinged open to display his wares and behind him a rough bed strewn with blankets held two sleeping children. The family cooked in the corner, and all their clothes hung on pegs or bulged out of a box at the end of the bed.

Sargento Jerez leaned on the horn and I was once again crunched between my two traveling companions for the last leg of the journey. Up the final hill, past cascading falls, water plummeted over rugged, shining rock, crashed onto the road before us, and flowed over its earthen surface into the valley below. At the top of the grade, kilometer 64, we looked back to the east over thickly verdant hills and the snow-capped Andes. On a clear day we could look straight up and see the tallest of Pichincha's shear rock peaks. To the west, land fell away rapidly and fifty miles beyond, the Pacific Ocean lapped on sandy beaches.

Los Bancos was at kilometer 94 and the *casa comunal* at kilometer 113. The largest structure in the area, after months of work this "community house" was still not completed. Upon our arrival we could see the tall and grizzled Maestro through the open stud walls. He was stooped over his bench working on planks milled from the jungle trees, planing themby hand to a fine smoothness. On his head he wore a dark cap, styled somewhere between that of the Oakland A's and Chairman Mao's. His ears flapped out from beneath its rim and piercing eyes watched as we swung into the small drive. Arms relaxed to his sides, his erect body turned to face us as we piled from the vehicle. He was smiling as we entered and came toward us to ask about our ride and our health.

As he conversed with Oswaldo, he struck me as a man of knowledge and warmth, driven from the city by some unknown harshness, exiled here, at the farthest point of cultural penetration. Soiled jungle guise hid a remote past from the casual observer, only his keen questions and darting eyes alerted me to his thriving intelligence.

More than once I was the object of his quizzing mind. On this particular evening, he grilled me with a haughty insistence. We had been left alone in the cool night breeze, a single flame flickering over our solitary visages. Acrid pungency flowed from the top of a reused bottle: jungle trago, cane alcohol, filled its interior. We had taken a deck of cards and passed through several hands of the local game when El Maestro tweaked me with his first question.

"What are you doing here?" It was a question he had asked numerous times before.

"What do you mean, what am I doing here?" Having covered this subject on previous visits, I felt my irritation mount. "Do you want to know what I'm doing here in the jungle, or in Quito, or in Los Bancos, or in the world in general?"

"Just tell me what you're doing here."

"I don't understand what you mean."

"You don't understand me and I don't understand you, so what are you doing here?"

"No, I understand you. I know what you're saying."

"No you don't. You can't understand me and I can't understand you. I don't know what you're doing here and if you don't either, you ought to go home."

I attempted a smile and searched frantically for sympathy, but found none. Sharp eyes dragged me back to his solemn intent. I hesitated, feeling threatened. "I'm here to do an economic study on the Northwest of Pichincha for Acción Cívica." My voice edged toward hysteria. The wise old Maestro had me on the run.

"I can't understand a thing you're saying," he said shaking his head. "You don't understand me. You don't understand any of the people who live out here."

"Sure I do."

"No you don't. How could you possibly do an economic study of these people? What do you know of economics?"

"The study is straight forward. I can just use what I learned in college. It's not necessary that I know a lot about the people. I just have to know how the system works to make people better off."

"What do you know about making these people better off? You can't understand them and they can't understand you."

"Yes I can."

"What did you say? I can't understand you. We could talk all night and I still wouldn't understand you. Your whole reason for being here is completely absurd. You ought to pack up your bags and go home." With that he sauntered outside to pee. Being in no mood to continue the con-

You can't understand them and they can't understand you.

versation, I walked to my bed and climbed in for a needed night's rest

Crowing roosters flitting from rafter to rafter woke me in the gray light and cool mist of the jungle dawn. By this second day, I had become accustomed to the raw humidity that penetrated all levels of life in this deep tropical clime. Perspiration, road dirt, and mud pervaded my clothing and body, forming a unity and wholeness with the environment.

Already other bodies were up and moving. Both Oswaldo's and Sargento Jerez's beds were vacated and when I rose they were the only others up. I didn't see El Maestro and we drove down the road for toast and coffee before he arose from his neighboring shed. I wondered about our previous night's conversation as I sipped my charcoaled caffeine.

Acción Cívica's needs ordered our day and after breakfast the first priority was buying bananas to take back to the city. We drove west, to lower altitudes and lusher growth, on the new, finely-crushed marble road. Only one vehicle could fit within its width and we sped toward the sea, paralleling the equator, with little fear of meeting oncoming traffic. Bamboo huts and banana plants inserted into the jungle morass marked the side of the road, and as we neared the end, where tractors tangled with vines to further western man's penetration into the jungle, we stopped at a house Oswaldo knew would sell bananas.

Situated on a rise tens of yards off the main road, the house was made of heavy poles half-a-foot thick, lashed together with sturdy vines. *Pambil*, stalks of bamboo slashed lengthwise and flattened into broad sheets, formed the walls and floors. Long, broad leaves, browned in the sun, matching the *pambil* and logs, were stacked, thatched and woven across the roof. Most of the floor was open porch, with only one small room in the rear enclosed by walls. A hand-notched log served as a ladder spanning the meter from the ground to the raised floor. Beneath it, chickens spalked and balked among wallowing pigs. A child's cry came from the walled room.

A young man hailed us from beneath the fronds of a banana plant as we surveyed the scene. "Good morning, Señores," he greeted us. "How are you and how can I be of service to you?" Shorter than I, he wore mud-caked baggy pants that became whiter as they approached his waist. His shirt was splattered with soil, one of the sleeves rolled to the elbow, the other opened freely at his wrist. With skin the brown of the jungle, his clear face smiled and one eye locked on us while the other wandered to the sky, lost forever in a life without cures.

"Good day, Señor," Oswaldo responded, "how goes it with you this morning?"

"As goes life, so goes the morning."

"Listen," Oswaldo continued, "we are interested in buying some bananas and wonder if you would be so kind as to fetch us a few branches of your best."

"Gladly," he smiled. "Would you like to come and see?"

"No," Oswaldo assured him. "You go on ahead."

"Wait," I interjected, "I want to go see."

Surprised, the man twisted around. "The mister? Does the mister know the banana plant?"

"Not well," I admitted.

His eyes lighted up, "You've come to the right place. We have lots of bananas. Ecuador is pure banana. Here, follow me."

I did, through tall grasses, behind his house to a hillside of the sinuous fruit. Banana stalks rose a dozen feet from the ground. Great veined leaves extended toward the sky over older ones drooping and falling to the earth, allowing brilliant red blossoms to bloom into bulging branches of bananas.

A slight breeze set their broad leaves gently dancing, while the cracked and aged branches brushed against our heads. At our feet, new shoots, slender cylinders of life, burst from the earth, unfolding leaves as if they were blankets wrapped carefully about newly born babies.

Watching the man and his environment brought back thoughts of my economic study and the previous night's harangue by El Maestro. "Tell me," I asked, "how many bananas do you grow?"

"Oh, mister, we have lots of bananas, many, many, many bananas. My father and I work this land and we have lots of bananas"

"Where do you sell them?"

"Well, we can't sell them all. We mainly sell to the man that comes down the road with his truck and buys bananas from everybody."

"Only one man buys all the bananas around here?"

"Uh huh, that's right."

"Why don't more come?"

" Oh, I think they have an agreement. They figure they can buy them cheaper if only one man comes, so that's the way they do it."

"Well, if you can't sell all of your bananas at a good price, why don't you raise something else? Rice, or something your family can eat?"

"We raise a little coffee and cacao, but we can't really eat it. They are not very good food. I could grow rice but I don't know how. We *costeños* have always grown bananas, coffee and cacao and bought our food in the store."

"You don't have to do that you know," I told him. "In fact all you're doing is making the middlemen and retailers, who ship your products and sell them in my country, a little wealthier along the way. Basically you're providing cheap food for my country. I bet you could grow your own food and be pretty self-sufficient right here."

Widening his one eye, sweat dripping from his brow in the intense jungle heat, my host asked, "Do you mean, mister, if I didn't grow bananas for the people of your country to eat, then I could grow my own rice and not sell my stuff to the man that comes down the road?"

"That's the idea," I told him.

From his side he pulled a long, glistening machete. Raising it above his head he grunted, "Well," whack! and down came a 100-pound branch of bananas, "I would certainly rather grow rice for my family than sell these god-awful bananas so incredibly cheap. But," whack! "I don't think I could save enough money to keep my family alive during the time I would need to learn how to grow the stuff." Whack! "But it sure would make sense if I did." Whack!

Throwing one branch over his shoulder and dragging another by its thick stalk, he signaled for me to bring the third. Trying to lift it, I collapsed under the weight. Reduced to dragging the branch with both hands, I used all the strength I could muster. By the time I reached the road, Oswaldo had negotiated the purchase and the two other branches were in the back of the pickup. We thanked the man and, back in the cab, I asked Oswaldo how much I owed him for my branch of bananas.

"Well, it was a lot of money, *Zhamez*," he smiled. "Three *sucres* for a branch, two hundred bananas. Those poor suckers, they aren't ever going to make it in this world!"

Back in Quito I wrote-up a proposal for an economic study of the "zone." The first order of business was to outline what resources existed in the zone and who owned them. When I presented this to Oswaldo, he frowned. "I don't think El Mayor is going to like this. You want to know who owns all the land in the zone? Most of the cooperatives are formed by military and ex-military people. At least they control the land along the road. Off the road, like in Pachijal, there are some people who own their own land but I don't know if they have land titles."

Startled, I protested, "But how about all those people living out there? They aren't military types."

"Oh, I know," he responded. "But they don't own the land. They just work there. It's better that way."

An American
Presence

MY JUNKYARD REFUGE didn't last. Even here I could not escape the American world. Besides the Americans who came to stay with me, there were Americans both downhill and uphill from me.

Scott Cooper, another Peace Corps type, lived on the steep Guapolo hillside below me in another group of apartments leased to Americans by the acquisitive Virginia Vivar. Scott and I shared similar lives, growing up in the great Northwest, attending school in Washington, DC while working at the US Capitol and now living on this Guapolo hillside. We formed an easy bond and I shared many adventures with him, enjoying his quick smile and easy way.

On the other side of my home across a field at the top of the hill sat another American presence, an American institution of immenseeconomic and political influence, perhaps the greatest in Ecuador, or for that matter, the world. It was housed in a mysterious, square, three-story blue structure that had been converted from a home into a veiled office building. Neither sign nor nameplate violated its anonymity. Only a blue-uniformed guard, stationed in front of a glass entry distinguished the building from its neighbors. For some time, however, I had been aware that activities at this locale had a flavor apart from the Ecuadorian norm. Black Mercedes limousines with tinted windows delivered finely dressed gentlemen to its portal, leaving serious and officious chauffeurs lingering by the curb. Past the first glass entry I could see a second uniformed guard checking visitors in and out of the edifice. Behind that guard, an opaque wall blocked all workings of the deeper interior from view.

Across the street a small coterie of personnel kept a close watch on this building as they did all activities in the area. Here as long as buses ran, from sunrise to past sunset, sat a slight, elderly man, whose neck rose from an oversized gray coat in a series of emaciated tendons that controlled the bobbing and weaving of his lean skull. He sold candy, penny sweets to the passengers of the #13 Hotel Quito-Chaguarquingo bus, which had its northern terminus at this particular corner. On a day of slow buses and growing curiosity, I asked the old vendor of tiny confections what he knew of the house across the way.

"Oh, now Mister," he stammered, raising his bowed head from his tray of sugared goods, "I don't know much about that."

This innocent fellow had to know more than he let on. He scrutinized every visitor who entered and left. He had constant run-ins with the guard and he overheard dozens of conversations between visitors there.

"You spend all your time watching that place," I said. "After all these years, you must know what is going on inside."

His sly smile returned and his head bowed again. "Well," he ventured, "all I know is what the guard and my customers tell me. They say it's an American Oil Company, but being an Americano, you must know that."

Startled, I paused before responding, "An American oil company! No, I didn't know that. But it makes sense." Actually it was the most obvious of answers. The oil companies were well established in Ecuador and had been for some time. Their exploits, however, had not made them popular and now, as they pumped over 200,000 barrels of crude oil a day out of the

Amazon basin far to the east, they apparently wanted to keep a low public profile to shield themselves from any public interference with their project.[1]

I knew of the oilmen, because I had been to their haunt, a secretive little bar just over the hill. I frequented this spot they called El Vaquero to get a little taste of something from back in the States. It was located amid embassies, winding streets, old colonial mansions, broad boulevards and massive modern homes. It occupied the interior of one of the latter on the corner of a broad boulevard and a narrow, curving street. No other commercial establishment shared its location. The windows were covered and once past color-paned doors, the visitor entered the land of the North. To the right, swinging doors led to a dine-and-dance space, while a long bar backed by bottles and American memorabilia took up the rear. Low captain's chairs surrounded a dozen small tables and rough wooden planks covered the walls. It reminded me of a barn just outside El Paso: cow horns and country western music completed the scene.

It was here that the riggers, fitters and dredgers escaped from the "gookland" outside its walls. In the past several years, they had come in droves from an array of Texas firms to take out oil for Americans back home. They laughed at their Ecuadorian hosts and told jokes at their expense. "Gooks," was the term they used for the spinners of wool and marketers of survival who carried on their lives in the Andean mountains. Like the draftees who popularized that term during another American invasion far to the east, few of these conscriptees or their families were here by choice, but rather for duty and pay.

Lack of choice led to lack of spontaneity and caring, creating a sorrow-

---

[1] Certainly the controversy they stirred gave the oil companies good reason to maintain a low profile. Trouble began in the 1920s as Leonard Exploration Company laid the groundwork for oil dealings in Ecuador when they denied that they were part of Rockefeller's Standard Oil, though, in fact, they were. Twenty years later, a squabble between Standard and Shell helped fan the flames of the 1941 war between Ecuador and Peru which still flares up over the border in the eastern *(Oriente)* jungle. (All Ecuadorian maps still show a vast region of the Amazon as Ecuadorian, although most maps in the US show this region as Peruvian..) In 1949, the oil companies formed a consortium, informed the Ecuadorians and Peruvians that there was no oil in the Amazon and closed down operations. In 1969 theyrevealed that their earlier statements were false by opening up hundreds of new productive wellsin the Amazon. In June 1971, there were twenty-one US corporations searching for oil in the *Oriente* and an additional number constructing a 321-mile pipeline over the 13,000 foot Andes Mountains.

ful scene. Large, drawling ladies, white skin sagging heavily off their arms, shared tables with gangly, six-foot men wearing pointed-toed cowboy boots. Elbows rested beside half-drunk beers. A raucous laugh or slow smile covered their faces. Shouting and threats came from the bar.

One afternoon I heard two of the loose-skinned women talking of their plight, of the "low-paying" jobs, and their inability to get by.

"I don't know Mabel, how we can do it. We only get fifteen thousand cash and that's barely enough. Of course the house is all paid for and so is the school, but honestly, I don't know how we can get by."

Fifteen thousand dollars, the sum boggled my mind. I received only two and lived like a king. As for their houses, I knew where they were, out in the northern suburbs where I had once lived. Their men, however, usually weren't home, but rather away in the Amazon sucking oil from beneath the jungle floor.

Scott once told me he had had a run-in with one of these lonely ladies on New Year's eve at El Vaquero. "I got manhandled by some rigger's woman," is all he would tell me but I knew by his tone that it was quite an adventure.

This was not his only investigation into the world of oil-drilling, however, and he figured his other investigation would award him a prize worth keeping. With luck maybe it would even garnewr him a Pulitzer.

Arriving in Ecuador as an independent traveler in early 1973, Scott had persuaded the local Director to hire him as editor of the Peace Corps newspaper *Intercom*. Once installed in this job and true to his activist spirit, he nosed around Ecuador for various stories worth publishing.

Testimonials by volunteers that appeared in *Intercom* in October 1972 were his first clue that something was awry with oil drilling in the Oriente. Lago Agrio, 100 miles east of Quito, beyond the eastern range of the Andes and down into the Amazon jungle bottoms that feed the world's mightiest river system, was the center of the oil development. This was a part of the planet that Western man had never conquered. The lure of oil, however, was changing all that. As these volunteers reported, "Air pollution in the Lago Agrio area defies belief. A solid covering of oil waste to coat every water supply in the area."

Pumping more oil out of the ground than they could process, the oil companies channeled the overflow, which "can run into hundreds of barrels at a time," into earthen pits, which were then ignited. "The burning is done day and night, day after day," the volunteers affirmed, "and since the prevailing winds come from the Amazon basin to the east, the huge black billowing clouds, which on a sunny day will block out the sun, hang perpetually over the town. The damage comes with the rains and since this is an area which receives well over 100 inches a year, the damage is not small. The cloud of smoke, being heavy with carbon particles, is blown low over the town. The rain comes and brings the clouds down to earth, covering everything underneath with a huge oil slick, people, animals, vegetation, and above all, the water supply."[2]

Writing in 1974, Scott continued their story with a series of photos showing smoke billowing over the jungle. He wrote, "The burnings have not stopped. Pictures taken for *Intercom* by a former Texaco technician show that as of March '74 oil burnings are taking place at, at least, three separate production sites.

"Everyday more and more oil goes up into the air as smoke and down again with the rains as pollution. Oil production on the Rio Napo, the Aguarica and other tributaries of the Amazon threaten the natural purity. These burnings and the resulting pollution could be avoided at a slightly greater cost to Texaco by the building of lined storage pits that would collect the excess oil and hold it for future recycling. . ."[3]

Meanwhile, in those days of oil shortages back in the States, as Americans were spending hours in line getting gas for their cars, Scott noted that Maurice F. Granville, then CEO and Chairman of the Board of Texaco, was making speeches to American audiences saying "we must implement the lower levels of gasoline deliveries, the Saturday night and Sunday ban on gasoline sales, the reduction of speed limits, the tightening of jet aircraft schedules, the dimming of ornamental outdoor lighting and the cut-back on deliveries of home-heating oil." Granville also assured his audiences that, "We in the industry are now proceeding as individual companies to cope with the problem [the shortage of petroleum] in the best ways we know how, despite false accusations and attacks from all sides . . . We must overcome the wasteful habit of using energy like water in a rain-

---

[2] Steve Troyanovich and Kevin Kingsfield, *Intercom* October, 1972.

[3] Scott Cooper, *Intercom* March 1974.

storm . . . We are going to be part of the solution, not part of the problem."[4]

Meanwhile, out in the Amazon, Texaco burned hundreds of barrels a day of high-grade crude oil, destroying the Amazonian environment in the process.

Writing again in *Intercom* Scott pointed out that, "When there has been oil damage in highly visible areas such as Santa Barbara, oil companies have gone to great expense to assuage the angry natives. But back in Ecuador, when the filth covers the drinking water and floats down the river rather than covering expensive beaches, the potential disaster to the environment is seen merely as a problem for an accountant to settle, i.e. 'what's cheapest?' And, so the 'problem' well . . . it just goes up in smoke."[5]

* * *

Finally, twenty years later, Scott's dream of this issue coming to the world's attention has begun. Unfortunately the situation has deteriorated in that time. A release from Rainforest Action Network in 1993 states, "It is crucial that we hold Texaco responsible for cleaning up its mess. . . The impacts of Texaco's presence [in the Ecuadorian Oriente] has been well documented: thirty major oil spills dumping seventeen million gallons of crude oil into the river systems of the Amazon (50% more than the Exxon Valdez disaster); discharges of twenty billion gallons of toxic chemicals; hundreds of toxic waste ponds abandoned; construction of a network of roads causing the colonization and deforestation of nearly two million five hundred thousand acres of tropical rainforests displacing Quichua, Cafan and Huaroni native peoples; causing ill-health effects among Indigenous peoples and small farmers including malnutrition caused by pollution of fishing grounds, headaches, skin and gastrointestinal illnesses and cancer."[6]

---

[4] Maurice F. Granville in speeches before the Independent Natural Gas Association of America on September 18, 1973, and the Rotary Club of Atlanta on November 26, 1973.

[5] Scott Cooper, "Intercom," March 1974.

[6] "Ecuadorian Indigenous People, Environmental Activists Call For International Boycott Of Texaco," *Peace Net* Rainforest Action Network, August 5, 1993.

Robert F. Kennedy, Jr. and the Natural Resources Defense Council negotiated a deal with the CONOCO Oil Company for CONOCO to contribute ten million dollars to a newly created non-profit institution that would benefit the indigenous people of the Oriente in exchange for NRDC's blessings on a project CONOCO is undertaking in the area. Unfortunately the NRDC made the same mistake Acción Cívica had made in the Northwest of Pichincha Province. They never talked to the people living there. When they were finally asked, the Huaroni didn't want the money. They just wanted the American presence to go away.

Pachijal

Away to a world
  undreamed of before
A spot by the river,
  a clearing, no more.
Residence in life
  their wisdom best known.
Although I came solo,
  I came not alone.

A TUNNEL FORMED by a canopy of heavy trees spiralling up multitudinous meters, intertwining leafy wings with neighboring branches, created the connection between two worlds. Succulent vines, climbing thick trunks, lofted themselves skyward to drop slender flowers with scarlet petals and sinuous yellow tongues.

Five deep ravines plagued the beginning of the path to Pachijal, each with a rushing creek to be forded. I had crossed them before with people from Pachijal, certainly I could manage them by myself. Halfway across the third, I was in trouble as water rose past my waist. I couldn't see the bottom for the splashing of the rapids. It got deeper in the next step. I looked for a lifeline, a means of support. Only a thin branch offered aid. I couldn't go back; there was no assistance there. No humans would miss me. One wrong step and I was gone. Any cries of panic would be lost to the trees and the birds.

Three feet below water, my rubber boots clung to rocks. Grasping the solitary branch, I inched forward, feeling with my lead foot for a solid hold. Water came higher, to my chest. My line of survival strained from its source. Bringing the trailing foot even, I searched along the bottom for a secure stone. Current pushed on my body. I got a firm hold and tugged on the branch until I found another step. Water receded to my waist and then to my knees as I emerged on the far side of the stream.

On solid ground I turned for a look at my innocent foe. How had the people of Pachijal done it? I couldn't understand. Seventeen kilometers along this path, through these raging streams, they had carried construction material — concrete, rebar and steel beams — for a schoolconstruction project in Pachijal I had become involved with.

Eight months earlier, at their request, I had undertaken a program to find money to build the school. A middle-school south of Seattle raised the money through cookie sales and Acción Cívica organized and delivered the materials to the trailhead. The people of Pachijal may have thought it was a great idea, but I wasn't too sure. It wasn't to education that I objected, rather the kind of memorization and socialization that came with it.*

Hard, slick, gooey mud marked the route up the next hill. I slid back on every step. Once on the plateau, hard turned to soft and I sank up to my knees in muck. Here I encountered the only other travelers I met that day: a young man leading a woman perched side saddle on a mule. He wore the attire of the jungle, a thin, sweat-stained cotton shirt, dirt spattered pants and rubber boots.

Past them and alone I came to a "Y" in the trail. Heading to the right, the land sloped away. My route took on such a steep angle that it was easier to slide and I bumped on my rear a thousand feet to the trail's bottom.

---

* I remember sitting in a one-room wooden schoolhouse at kilometer 122. which had windows but no glass. There were six grades and twenty desks. Pupils came from families without formal educations. Most of the mothers had one set of clothes, rubber boots and groomed their black hair with a part in the middle. On the wall of the school, however, hung a poster of a made-up, blond woman with coiffured hair; below it was the word "Mamá." I shook my head, that wasn't any Mamá these children knew.

Although I came solo, I came not alone.

Pachijal

There the Pachijal River, broader than the creeks, ran through a wide valley flatland where I stopped for a rest. It was here on our first journey, when Robert Ladine was still with me, that we had collapsed from exhaustion, unable to go on.

We had been saved on that day by some families on the far side of the river who fed and gave us a chance to rest before lending us two mules for the remainder of our journey. Big blond Bob gave them a speech that day that made them all gawk, and I imagine to this day, we white men are something they still haven't forgotten. Now there were no signs of life, however, and I shook my head thinking what a spectacle we must have been.

My journey was half over, and I followed the river downstream. I walked for hours through solid, sheeting, drenching tropical rains — "making winter," as they say in the jungle. Eventually *pambil* houses bordering a clearing came into view — Pachijal.

Residents moved quietly about their bamboo homes. I discerned shadows within neat picket-railed porches beneath the heavy brows of thatched roofs. No sound broke the silence save the caw of the birds, macaws and parrots in the tops of the trees.

Rafael spotted me across the open field. Not a native of Pachijal, he was black-skinned and hailed from Santo Domingo de los Colorados on the main road to the coast. He, the Ministry of Education's teacher, and a few colonists who had come in from the mountains were the major instigators and hardest workers behind the school project.

I was sitting on my backpack in the downpour, still resting, when he reached me. "Good afternoon Mr. Jim, welcome," he shook my hand. "When you didn't come before Christmas, I didn't think you would be here till after the first of the year."

Recovering from my trek, I responded slowly. "Good afternoon, I am here now."

Scrunching up his forehead he asked, "Did you come alone?"

"I certainly did," I assured him, beginning to regain my strength.

"That's a long trip," he said somewhat in wonderment that this gringo should attempt such an escapade on his own.

"It wasn't so bad," I tried to assure him.

"Good, good," he said, somewhat relieved. "Do you have plans to stay a couple of days? Partake in the New Year with the people of Pachijal?"

"Uh huh, that would be nice," I responded.

"Oh that would be great my friend, but do you have a place where you will stay?," he asked.

"I think I'll sleep over in that unfinished building where I stayed before, if that is all right," I answered.

"That was Enrique's building, huh? He's using that building now, maybe you'd better sleep in the church. That would be a good spot."

Indeed, the church was a secure spot and a reminder that I had been beaten to this jungle locale by Padre Bernabé, the walking priest of the jungle. While almost all the buildings in this clearing were made out of traditional *pambil* bamboo, the church was built with planks and a tin roof, and its wooden benches made as fine a bed as could be found in Pachijal.

"And you'll take meals with Alfonso and Alicia?" Rafael asked.

"Sure, if they'll have me," I said. "In fact I think I'll go up there right now. I left some clothes there and I'd like to change."

"Right, good," Rafael smiled, "I think Alicia is there. She'll take care of you. We'll see you later Mister. It'll be an honor to have you here for our New Year's celebration."

Behind the row of pambil homes surrounding the clearing, I trudged up a hillside that reached into the low hanging clouds. In a small home nestled at the threshold of the encroaching tangle of trees and vinese lived the man known as Alfonso with his wife Alicia and their three small daughters.

I halted a few yards in front of their residence. Like the others in Pachijal, it was lifted off the ground by piers, pairs of six-inch thick poles, bound with heavy jungle fibers. I gave a call to see if anyone was about besides the few chickens that scratched in the mud. Steps came from the back and Alicia, black hair frizzed, a grave expression on her young face, stepped to the porch. "Hello mister, what a surprise!," she greeted me.

"Buenas tardes, Alicia," I returned her greeting. "As you can tell, I have once again arrived and am wondering if I may partake of meals with you and your family for the next few days?"

"But of course, Mister," she said. "Does Alfonso know you're here?"

"No, not yet. I haven't seen him. I just arrived."

"Oh, he'll be so excited. The men have been working hard to get all the materials for the school here. It takes five men to carry one of those beams."

Thinking about the trail I had just traveled, I marveled, "I can't believe they did it. It's hard for me just to walk it."

"Well, you must be tired, Mister, if you just made that trip. Please come in and I'll fix you something to drink. I think you left some clothes here. You should come up and change. Whew, is it ever making winter these days!"

"That it is," I agreed, as I climbed the notched log leading up to the porch where she gave me my clothes and then went back to her open-air cooking area behind the house.

I was dressed and seated at their rough-hewn table on the porch looking over the gentle jungle scene when she returned with a glass of fresh lemon juice and a little sugar cane; the best lemonade I ever had. She watched as I drank.

"Did it take you a long time to come on the trail?," she asked.

"Five hours maybe, not as long as before."

"And you came alone?"

"Right," I paused and then looking at her asked, "do you think that was a dangerous thing to do?"

"Dangerous? Well, I don't know. Why, were the rivers high?"

"Well, yes, the rivers were high. In fact I was almost swept away in one creek. But besides that, are there any dangerous animals out there? I didn't even have a machete."

Shaking her head she said, "No, I don't think that there are any dangerous animals out there."

"Oh good," I said, "no poisonous snakes or anything?"

Then skewing her face into a thoughtful mode she said, "Well, huh. There might be snakes. My brother-in-law at his place over on the river killed a snake about the size of this log here," pointing to a six-inch thick, twenty-foot long pole, "only a few weeks ago."

"Is that right," I stiffened slightly. "Poisonous?"

"Poisonous, terribly poisonous, extremely poisonous," she shook her head.

"How did he kill it?" I asked.

"With his machete."

Startled by this revelation I asked, "So, are there any other animals around?"

Thinking again she nodded. "Well, my father, about six months ago, shot a leopard in his corral."

"A leopard! How big?"

"Oh, about the height of this table."

"Are there many of those around?" I asked in amazement.

"A few I guess."

"Huh, good thing I didn't run into anything," I muttered, imagining the beasts I could have encountered along the lonely trail.

"It certainly is," she concurred.

I fell silent in thought gazing at the scene. I was in an environment unlike anything I had known before. People existed on a different level of awareness with their surroundings. They had no fear of circumstances which seemed incredibly perilous to me. They survived on foods grown in the area. Only cows could be walked to the road for sale. I sat for several minutes staring about me before excusing myself and telling Alicia I would return before dark. Exhausted, I slipped down the hill to the church for a nap before dinner.

Alfonso had returned home and greeted me there when I again climbed the hill, this time as the world disappeared into the black obscurity of night. He was a young fellow with thin brows arching high above dark inquisitive eyes. Puffy cheeks ran back to meet elephantine ears flapping out over thick dark hair. We exchanged greetings and shared a meal of rice and sauce while his wife and daughters ate in the rear kitchen. A lighted wick, stuck in a small bowl of kerosene, sputtered in the cool evening breeze and illuminated the rounded features of Alfonso's face as he spoke. "The *Consejo* (Provincial Government) says they are going to put a road into Pachijal. What do you think about that?"

"A road? From where?" I asked.

"From kilometer 104."

"Are they going to do that soon?"

"Right away."

Pausing, I thought about this new development for a moment. "Well, that's going to change your town quite a bit," I told him.

"Do you think it will change it for the good or the bad?" he asked.

Thinking of the military and the system of land cooperatives in the rest of the area, I inquired if the people living in Pachijal had official land titles.

"No, not yet, but we're working on them," he told me.

"Well, if you don't have land titles and the road comes in here, people will come in and buy all the land or at least get title to it, because they know the rules of the government bureaucracy and have friends in the right places who can help them form cooperatives. Of course, they might come in and get your land without a road, but with a road it's almost a sure thing that someone will at least try to do that, particularly if you don't have secure titles. Then, instead of being farmers, you'll be workers for someone else."

"Yeah," he nodded, "but wouldn't it be nice to have trucks coming in here and taking our crops to Quito to sell?"

"Well, as I say, you may be the one growing it, but you're not necessarily going to be the one selling it. If you lose your land, you're going to have to work hard for somebody else to earn the money to feed your family. Life will become expensive and arduous. Those trucks will make noise and muck up your clearing. I am not thinking that a road is such a good thing."

His expression fallen, Alfonso lamented, "The men around here, we have talked about those things but don't know what we can do. How do we change the *Consejo*? Fighting and revolution, which is maybe the only other choice, is very dangerous."

Contemplating the grave situation these people found themselves in, I could only sympathize, "It is truly not a nice choice," I said. "But one thing you can do is make sure you legally own your land."

"We'll see if we can do that," he assured me.

Realizing that my time in Ecuador was coming to an end, I was at a loss to offer him any more assistance. I didn't understand the machinations of the Ecuadorian bureaucracy and could not accurately predict what would happen when a road reached Pachijal. "Work on it," I encouraged him. "Now, I'm going to bed. I'll see you in the morning." Taking a flashlight I had brought, I climbed to the ground and wound down the hill to the church.

Gray clouds still encompassed the town the next morning as I climbed the hill for breakfast. Alfonso was already gone, but Alicia had kept the morning meal hot for me on her coal grill.

"Last day of the year Mister," she said. "Are you going to stay for our New Year's celebration?"

"I plan on it, if that would be all right. Is it going to be quite a fiesta?"

"It should be. We'll burn the stuffed dummy and then there'll be dancing and music." Walking to her porch to overlook the entire town she said, "It should be quite a good time."

"I look forward to it," I told her, but she was lost in thought as she gazed at the town.

"Didn't you stay at that building of Enrique's last time you were here?," she asked.

"That's right."

"I don't understand why one man needs so many buildings as that Enrique. He has a house on the ridge, a house here in town and now he has that new building."

"What's he use them all for?"

"I don't know," she said. "His wife and daughter live on the hill. I think he wants to rent his house in town and now he's making his new building into a store. What's one man need so much for?"

"I don't know," I said. "It's definitely a problem. What kind of a store is he putting in? I didn't think there were any stores here in Pachijal."

"Just a store with sodas and beer and candy and such. I don't understand," she said shaking her head.

"How does he get supplies here?" I asked.

She didn't answer, but climbed down the log to do some chores outside. I finished my breakfast and decided to go exploring around town to investigate the essence of life in Pachijal.

Still being a stranger — white skin, Levi's and all — I felt awkward and decided to go to the river beyond the clearing. There the Río Pachijal bounded between boulders towards the Río Guayllabamba which took it into the sea forty miles away. Lush growth enveloped the banks of the Río Pachijaland I stretched on a sun-cleansed rock to contemplate the swirling water.

Tiring of this, I searched along the bank and then returned up the slope to the houses. Noticing some decayed structures by the church I went to investigate. No one watched or cared about my activities and my tensions faded. The melody of the river filled the clearing along with the chatter of the birds in the jungle trees. They formed a unity, a wholeness. I leaned against a fading grass wall to observe, feel, become a part of it all.

My eyes rested on the nearest house and its occupants. Large in comparison to others, it still only had one enclosed room. A scurry of activity surrounded it. Tiny tots chased one another, older ones stirred pots and several men worked at projects on the ground. On the step leading from the soggy earth to the raised floor sat a plumpish woman directing activities on all side. She wore a gray smock patched, sewn and pinned with bright red cloth in spots of disintegration. Her hands flurried about a reed basket she was creating on her lap. Beside her sat one already completed. Using dried grass half-an-inch wide, she wove a netting incorporating lateral rings to give it shape. Her fingers jumped between a dozen separate reed ends in the process. Upon completion it was half a meter wide by one meter tall and when lined with broad jungle leaf made a strong pack that could be lashed onto a person's back.

She was watching me and gave a call, "Say Mister, would you like to come have some coffee?"

Startled, I paused. "Why, thank you, I would like some coffee," I answered. Strolling to the steps, I sat down below her.

"How are you today Mister?," she asked. "How do you like our little town?"

"It's beautiful!" I exclaimed. "How long have you lived here?"

"Many years," she responded, "I'm the sister of the woman who fixes your meals there in the house on the hill. Our brother lives in that house over there and our parents live on a small farm just down the path." Then turning to a small girl said, "Maria, bring the Mister a cup and some coffee."

She addressed a shy girl with hair tied back wearing a simple cotton dress. The coffee came in a blackened tin and she handed it to her mother who passed it to me.

"You grow this coffee yourselves?" I asked.

"We do, or some of us grow coffee. We all do what we can. This coffee comes from the farm of my parents. How do you like it?"

"Very good," I assured her. "You seem to have a pleasant life."

"A pleasant life?" Perplexity crossed her face. "This is life. There isn't any other. We raise our animals, grow our food. The boys work with the men and the girls do their chores. Life is good; there is no other."

Silent, I thought of the school, the impending road, the creeping expansion of the World economy.

New Years Eve flowed with harmony. They stuffed a dummy, an effigy, a representation of the year gone by. As the final moments passed, they read a list of events, humorous stories and tragic mishaps that had occurred to all the residents of the town in the past year. Even the "coming of the Mister" was mentioned. As they read, the dummy burned. As the year ended, the list burned too. It was over, done, eulogized, buried and forgotten. Now was the time to celebrate and they did: music, *trago*, dancing, fun for everyone.

I snuck back to the church and sleep before dawn. Few others did. They slept as I woke and left, never to return. My presence, however, foreshadowed a change to their tranquil life.

Legitimacy

*The state or quality of conform-
ing to recognized principles or
accepted standards.*

L EGITIMACY IS A CONCEPT THAT HAUNTS Americans. As
our consumption instigates pollution of the the Amazon and under-
mines traditional values around the world, our legitimacy is something we have to come to terms with. Back in Ecuador in early 1975 the
concept of legitimacy surfaced in my brain and depressed my heart: depres-
sion not over legitimacy, but its opposite, non-legitimacy. A year in the
jungle as a PR man for America and the Ecuadorian Ministry of Defense
deposited me in a state of dejection, debating my own legitimacy.

With a flick of his hand Cristóbal Gutiérrez, a young-man-in-a-hurry
Latino style, helped me launch a study of my legitimacy and that of all the
do-gooders doing whatever they did in Ecuador. Tall, handsome and
aggressive, sporting an impish mustache and thin smile, he was Assistant

Director of the Peace Corps in Ecuador. To my astonishment he suggested we do an investigation of the legitimacy of Peace Corps, the United States Agency for International Development (USAID); of all foreign aid entering Ecuador. I am not sure why he suggested it. Maybe he had doubts about his own role. Perhaps he wanted to use the findings in a doctoral dissertation. I wasn't certain. I didn't care. I liked the idea.

He contributed a stack of source materials which I accepted and carried home for perusal. One of these, a United Nations' study, revealed an array of disturbing facts concerning foreign aid. For example:

— Of the $11,000,000 Uncle Sam annually spent in Ecuador in the early sevcenties, $449,000 went for "collaboration in the maintenance of an adequate atmosphere for foreign aid and national investment and of the law and order necessary for the society in general." Quite a sum for Uncle Sam to be investing in a poor country's domestic police force. Cars, guns, new uniforms, sixteen scholarships to study in the United States. It reminded me of the movie *State of Siege*, and the International Police Academy in Washington DC, teaching terror and torture tactics to South American police and military to keep the people in their place and the economy open to the corporate overlords.

— $405,000 in one year to control narcotics, in a country that didn't use them.

— Little of this money was ever spent in Ecuador; it was spent almost entirely on salaries for experts from the US or for equipment purchased from US corporations. I began to wonder if the term "aid" was appropriate; whether it was "legitimate."

Reading, studying, philosophizing, and theorizing, I dove into the topic with relish. As I wrote, talked and organized the material, my thoughts began to crystallize. My project became known and people came to chat, give their views and tell me their experiences.

Nancy Kravenor was large, not just big, but large and full of smiles. I ran into her one day while collecting my mail in the Peace Corps lounge. A nurse serving in the southern reaches of Ecuador, she was in Quito to negotiate a $5,000,000 loan from USAID. That caught my attention, so I asked her to elaborate. Flopping into an overstuffed chair, she explained: "It's a paramedic program. We go into the countryside and give a six-week course on basic medicine. Young girls from the local villages take the course and then go back to their villages and establish *boticas* or basic pharmacies and medical centers."

I nodded, "So what's the loan for?"

"Well," she continued, shifting in her seat, "we don't have any money. The loan is to set up a joint program among the Ministry of Health, the Medical School at the University of Cuenca, Peace Corps and USAID. Right now, when the girls go back to their villages they can't get any medicines and no one in their town has money to pay them, so they can't be supported and the effort's all wasted. With the loan the girls could receive a small salary and have some drugs to treat their patients. Our hope is that the Ministry of Health will make it a national program."

"And how go your negotiations?" I asked.

"Not well."

"How come?"

"Oh," she sighed, "USAID insists we include birth control in the courses and the University of Cuenca refuses to do any kind of birth control."

Confused, I asked, "Why's that?"

"Haven't you heard this argument?" she asked in amazement and then plunged on without waiting for me to clear the confusion from my face. "Birth control is genocide by the industrialized countries trying to control the size of the world's surplus labor force; keeping it down when it's not needed, letting it grow when it is; keeping the masses to a manageable size; keeping the lid on the number of possible revolutionaries; that idea."

Surprised by this twist in the traditional birth control argument I nodded. "That's quite an argument. Not one I've heard before."

"Well, it's a legitimate one," she said, "that's held by quite a few people, not to mention that evreyone is Catholic and against birth control anyway. The real tragedy is that with such a roadblock our project may never get off the ground."

Such conversations simply drifted into my life. Mac, Marcos in Spanish, came for a short stay in Quito and talked of his life in the indigenous Otavaleño village where he grew an organic vegetable garden.

"The *jefes* (bosses) want me to help them get electricity," he told me as we sat at my eating table sipping a beer and staring at the view.

"What? Electricity!" I said in amazement as I thought of the tranquil, independent life around Lago San Pablo. "What do they want that for and who's ever going to pay for it?"

Leaning back and rolling his eyes, Marcos continued. "Well, you know the main dirt road with the high *cabuya* plants that hide all the houses? The one where the bus goes? They just want it to run along there."

"Why?" I asked with the cynicism that had grown over my two years in Ecuador. "Is that where all the *jefes* live?"

Smiling and raising one hand in the air Marcos exclaimed, "You got it. They'd be the only people to get the electricity."

Still confused I asked, "So, why do they want electricity?"

"They're all weavers you know," Marcos pointed out, setting his beer on the table. "They've gotten into selling to the tourists at the Saturday morning market. So now they want electric light so they can weave at night, produce more *ponchos*, make more money."

With realization dawning I asked, "Do they earn their entire living from weaving?"

Marcos assented, "Pretty much so."

"And they don't do any self-sufficient agriculture anymore?"[1]

"Nope, not much."

In amazement I began thinking out loud. "So let's see. In the great marketing-trading game they spend a couple of weeks making a sweater that they wholesale to someone from the States for fifteen dollars. Freight and taxes may cost another five dollars and then someone like Marshall Fields imports them and sells them for sixty-five dollars. About a three hundred percent markup. Meanwhile, right down the aisle at Marshall Fields a transistor radio made in Taiwan sells for twenty-two-fifty, though it really probably only costs five dollars to produce. In Ecuador, however, after freight, customs and a few other people have stuck their finger into the pie, the radio costs forty-five dollars. So the family of weavers, who are now working all night need to make three sweaters to buy the transistor radio, which, by the way, they probably never thought they needed until

---

[1] Actually, in the early 1970s there was still an extensive indigenous economy separate from the capitalist market system in the Andes. At that time about 752,000 workers within this self-reliant economy working on 400,000 parcels averaging five acres each grew enough food to support a majority of the 2,500,000 indigenous people in the country. In achieving this they attained a level of productivity double the national average.

they heard the one in your house. Then if the three sweaters sell for a total of one hundred and ninety-five dollars and the producers get a radio worth five dollars, a myriad of other market-related institutions pick up an extra one hundred ninety bucks from transactions connected to the making of the three sweaters. In view of that it certainly does make financial sense for the Western economies to rope as many people into their game as they can, wouldn't you say?"

I finished with a triumphant smile for working my way through that web of relationships. Marcos went for another beer, but I asked him as he disappeared into the kitchen, "So, Marcos, where does the power come from?"

Reappearing with two more tall ones, he affirmed my worst fear. "Our friend Steve [who headed the Peace Corps involvement with INECEL, the Ecuadorian electrification bureaucracy] says that it almost all comes from foreign sources or revenues from the oil companies."

This made sense. Ecuadorians would not necessarily electrify their own country because they historically did not have any electrical appliances to plug in. They are now buying their appliances from the States, so, of course, Uncle Sam is assisting the electrification effort.

I checked this out and discovered that over a two-year period more than $65,000,000 had been pumped into Ecuador by eight foreign countries and two multi-lateral institutions with the purpose of furthering the electrification of this small Andean nation. Two thirds came from North America or institutions it dominated, mostly in the form of low-interest, easy-term loans.[2]

And there were others who talked to me. A fellow on the coast, for example, told me of organizing self-sufficient farmers into production cooperatives that moved them into the market system and increased their dependence on price and distribution factors that were far beyond their control.

An American named Clausen picked me up hitchhiking one day and

---

[2] The tragedy of these types of loans is that little of it ever enters the recipient country and what does goes to highly paid bureaucrats. Since the loans rarely increase productivity sufficiently to pay the loans off they must be repaid through inflation and austerity programs imposed by the IMF. This means that the poor work harder and receive less in order for the government to pay back loans that mainly benefit the bureaucrats and foreign corporations.

related how he was contracting with AID to teach the indigenous people of the mountains the niceties of American hygiene, of washing one's hands, preparing them for the onslaught of the white man and the diseases he brings.

My interchanges on this study often happened by chance. I was once casually relating the thrust of my work to a near stranger when he exploded, "You can't do that!"

Startled, I asked, "What do you mean I can't do that?"

"You can't go telling the Ecuadorian government about all the money coming into this country," he insisted, "not to mention telling them what it is for."

Perplexed, I repeated my question, "What do you mean?"

"Why, there are people in this country the government doesn't want to be helped. I know a cultural group, an indigenous people, who are now dependent on the *mestizos* and colonists, but who are getting some cattle from a European aid group to become self-sufficient. Hey, this is a government with its allegiances to the big landowners and aristocracy in Quito! They're not worried about legitimacy. They don't want these people to get any help. If they knew about this money coming in, they would stop it immediately. This aid stuff is big business. Are you sure the government wants you to do this study?"

"Well, we'll find out," I said.

I worked for months developing a proposal, getting the elements straight in my head. Cristóbal Gutiérrez managed some contacts at the newly established Departmento de Asistencia Técnica of the National Planning Board which had responsibility over all foreign aid entering the country. They, too, needed a study on the effects of foreign aid in Ecuador. It appeared our timing was right. In our excitement, we recruited two more Peace Corps members, Bea Walgren, a sharp, handsome woman with a background in research and analysis, and Donald Shark, a fellow who had been head of Peace Corps' business program for several years.

Our initial meeting with the Planning Board took place in an upper story of its modern cement headquarters, in the office of the Director of the department. Past his expansive desk, windows offered views in two directions over the low Quito skyline. Eight people were present, four from the Peace Corps, the Director and three economists from his department.

They all had read my proposal. They talked and jabbered and I picked up only portions of their conversation.

One of the economists did not like my proposal, one was noncommittal, the third, Oscar León thought the proposal had merit. The Director wasn't sure, but said he did need a study. He arranged to have Bea, Donald and me work in the afternoons with Oscar León to develop an appropriate format.

Oscar, young with a heavy black beard, spent his mornings teaching economics at the Central University, center of radicalism in Quito. On our first day together we squeezed between his desk and an exposed pillar that supported the building. Once we were settled, he began, "Now I think we ought to start with what the Ecuadorian government's philosophy was according to the five-year plan that is now in effect."

We all nodded our approval.

"I've been going through some of these books and have copied down what the government's philosophy was. For instance, in *The General Vision of the Plan*, they said, 'The defective and unsatisfactory functioning of the economy is due to its ties to the international order. . . . The control of exports has been concentrated in a few hands that have tied the national production to the international order. . . The fluctuation of exports has caused the historical crisis of the country . . . The concentration of control has oriented the behavior of the economy and deformed it. Control of the economy has to be internal rather than external. . . Problems to be attacked in reaching development are . . . dependency and subordination of the economy and the society to foreign centers, etc.' Anyway, these were the government's philosophies that we should use."

Oscar was definitely on the same track I was but I did have one question. "Excuse me, Oscar. How come you keep saying 'was' and 'were' the philosophies, as if they were in the past?"

"Well," he looked up smiling, "I figure these were the government's philosophies because they wrote them three years ago when they came to power. But since they haven't done anything about them they must not be their philosophies now. Therefore, I can't use anything but the past tense to describe them."

We used them to establish a methodology and questionnaire for the study. Five areas were selected for concentration: (1) economic dependence, (2) concentration of income, (3) regional disequilibrium, (4) underproduction and under-utilization of resources and (5) unemployment and underemployment.

We planned to quiz all foreign aid institutions on how their programs addressed these points. Initially we used the Peace Corps files to come up with data to test our hypothesis. Our conclusion: Peace Corps' major effort was to make the workers of Ecuador more efficient workers. Peace Corps did not reduce economic dependence on foreign powers, it did not reduce the concentration of income in a few hands, and it did not reduce unemployment.

I was through. After twenty-seven months in Ecuador, my time was up and I was going back to the States. I hoped that Oscar, Bea and a new volunteer would study the rest of the foreign aid institutions and come to their own conclusion about the legitimacy or non-legitimacy of foreign aid in Ecuador.

Months later Bea wrote me that some higher-ups on the Planning Board didn't like Americans working in their building; Bea and friends were out. Cristóbal Gutiérrez wrote after that saying he heard the National Planning Board had budgeted $5,000 to begin a study of the effects of foreign aid in Ecuador. Months after that I read of a palace coup overthrowing El Bombito and that a Navy Admiral from the coast was now the President. The new government didn't even pretend to be nationalist and revolutionary. My letters addressed to the National Planning Board were never answered.

Route Through the Southern Cone

Santiago

MARCH 1975, I'd had enough of the smiling-American-in-the-Latin-culture routine. My departure time had come and I knew it. My landlady greedily bought my chess game and pillows she had previously condemned as the heart of my debauchery and I mused that I would never understand her mind.

After many nights of celebration, friends pointed me in the direction of the Air France jet indicated on my ticket and I was off, happy to be headed home. Peering over a window rim of the blue-striped bird, I watched the Andes and Ecuador sweep by below. Mount Cotopaxi, 18,000 feet, over there the beautiful and graceful Mount Chimborazo, 20,000 feet and to the south Sanguay, 15,5 . . ., SOUTH? We were headed south and the US was north. Wasn't I going the wrong way?

Bad news. I fought my mind to a state of clarity. I saw two choices: either assault the cockpit or jump. Before making any rash decisions I checked my ticket. That proved fruitful. It said Santiago de Chile. I was on my way now. Was that smart?

Chile was in terrible shape, worse than Ecuador. In 1970 Chileans had elected Salvador Allende to the presidency on a platform that he would discreetly, democratically and non-violently withdraw Chile from its niche in the international market system that I had observed creeping its way through Ecuador.[1] It was not a popular decision with Uncle Sam, who cut off all credit and aid — except to the military and the opposition [2]— and covertly supplied up to $40,000,000 to wreak havoc on the Chilean economy, people and society. Three years later the US reaped its reward; the military took over in a blood bath that left 20,000 dead in the streets and put General Augustos Pinochet in the Presidency. Capitalism was restored to Chile.

As I soared south a year and a half later, this ruthless military regime was still in power. I mused whether by visiting Chile I ran the risk of being jailed (and who knew what else) since my curly hair was longer than the

[1] In the last several decades, Chile had been placed in the position of exporting copper and importing foodstuffs. In 1970, 80% of Chile's copper production was in the hands of two US corporations, Kennecott and Anaconda Copper. Anaconda Copper was receiving 80% of its world profits from Chile and according to the North American Congress on Latin America, "In the past sixty years. . . US copper companies operating in Chile have taken home profits equivalent to half the value of all the nation's assets accumulated over the past 400 years."

[2] What quantity of resources the US government invested to destabilize the Chilean political process is a matter of open debate and closed files. The history of large-scale US involvement goes back to 1964 when, according to the former US ambassador, up to 20 million dollars was spent covertly by the US to guarantee the defeat of Salvador Allende in the Chilean presidential election that year. Six years later, when a similar effort failed to stop Allende from receiving an overwhelming plurality of votes, US actions took on a different flavor. Failure of their next option, to prevail upon the Chilean military to take over before Allende took office, led to a September 15, 1970, meeting between President Nixon, Henry Kissinger, Attorney General John Mitchell and CIA Director Richard Helms. Unearthed later, Helms' notes of this meeting indicated that in order "to make the Chilean economy scream" there was "ten million available, more if necessary." It was to be a full time job using "the best men available." Exactly where that money went and what those "best men" did is a tightly held secret within the CIA. But US instigated covert actions appeared to range from buying off the local media, to financing a strike of Chilean truck owners and sponsoring urban terrorism in the streets of Santiago. Between the years 1971 - 1973 (the years Allende was in office) the Nixon administration cut off all aid to Chile except for $45,500,000 which they directed toward the Chilean military despite a US Congressional ban on such aid.

norm and I carried a pack on my back.[3] On the other hand resistance fighters might mistake me for a CIA operative and do me in for the evil role my country had played in the undoing of their democracy. Was this trip a good idea?

At this point there wasn't much choice.

Orange rays from the setting sun tinted our monstrous machine as we touched down at Pudahuel outside Santiago, a point as far south of the equator as San Diego, California is north. It was a balmy evening in the center of this long, narrow country that stretches north into deserts and south to frigid Tierra del Fuego. To the east, the Andes, and to the west, the Pacific restrict Chile's girth to 100 miles.

People crowded into the customs area as I fumbled along, stuffing books and underwear into various pockets of my backpack that had come apart on the trip south. While waiting for the lines through customs to shorten I wandered over to a glass-encased cashier to exchange twenty dollars for Chilean *escudos*.

Quite a process ensued, including the filling-out of forms, showing my passport, signing documents and finally the exchange. After handing the cashier a twenty dollar traveler's check he began pulling piles of bills out of multiple drawers: five blue ones, four red ones, eight purple ones, two wrinkled ones, more and more until there was a stack of money an inch high in exchange for my twenty dollars. Forty-eight thousand Chilean *escudos*! I muttered and mumbled to myself as I tried to figure out what I was going to do with all this paper.

The longer I stayed in Chile, the worse the situation became. Three weeks later, twenty dollars bought me an inch and a half stack of bills, 68,000 *escudos*. US economic advisors[4] who were assisting the military to restructure the Chilean economy back into an export/import-dependent

---

[3] The military remained in power until 1989 when General Pinochet reluctantly ceded to popular demands and left the Presidency but named himself supreme military commander for the rest of his life and made dark warnings about the politicians doing anything that might displease him.

[4] Milton Friedman and Arnold J. Harberger, both at that time at the University of Chicago, had been particularly active in redesigning the Chilean economy from one that could be largely self-reliant to one that was dependent on exporting to and importing from the industrialized countries. By redirecting production and cutting employment, they created an inflation rate that in two years changed the value of the Chilean *escudo* from 1/24 of a dollar to 1/6000 of a dollar.

mold apparently were not doing much for the health of the domestic Chilean economy except raising prices.

Wondering about this, I ambled back to my pack, pushing wads of bills into my pouches and wallets. Before me lay Chilean customs, the specter of the Chilean police and all the horror stories I had heard about them since they had ousted President Allende and taken over the government. Wearing green woolen uniforms and severe countenances, they barely scanned my bag before sending me on my way.

Out to the buses, I missed the first one and was chatting with a young Canadian couple, when a four-seat Fiat halted before us. An attractive young Chilean woman popped her head through the driver's window and spoke to us in elegant English.

"Would you like a ride into town?," she asked.

A ride into town? We were slightly confused and peeked around at the empty bus stop to see if she was talking to someone else.

"We're just waiting for the bus," replied the Canadian male, a large blustery blond fellow with a full wavy beard.

"No, you don't understand," she laughed. "We'll give you a ride into town. We're going right through the middle of it. Where are you going, to a hotel?"

"Yeah," he said, "we would like to go a hotel, but we don't know which one." Then turning to me he asked, "How about you?"

"Sure," I said, "I could use a ride to a hotel. But do you think there is enough room?"

"Of course there is," the driver broke in.

"But look at all our luggage," the Canadian woman pointed out.

Surveying the scene, the driver assured us that it would all fit in the trunk. Opening the door and jumping to the curb, she stopped before reaching the rear, saying, "Oh, my name is Elena Mendoza and this," bending over and pointing to a chicly dressed woman in the passenger's seat, "is my mother Ana Mendoza." We waved and introduced ourselves and Ana smiled a bright cheery grin. Then Elena opened the back door and continued, "And here are my two children, Pepito and Juanita."

We said hello, but they just stared back with big black eyes and quizzical grins.

We squeezed our bags into the trunk and then, opening the back door, the children tumbled to the front as the three of us squished into the back. Ana, after giving us a pleasant look over her shoulder, tugged at her daughter's sleeve asking in Spanish who we were. They talked for several minutes as Elena drove onto a freeway and we watched the scenery go by.

After they had chatted for a bit, Elena glanced back at us and said, "I have an idea. Instead of staying in a hotel, you could stay at my mother's house. It's quite large, and she lives all alone."

"What's that?," we asked, startled by the unexpected hospitality that was pouring forth from our new-found Chilean friends. "Stay with your mother? Is that what you said?"

"That's right. You could pay her a little something, less than a hotel."

"It's all right with her? She knows what you are offering?" I was amazed.

"Oh, she's the one who suggested it. She thinks it'd be fine."

"Well," I said, "I'm just staying for a few days. That would be nice for me."

"Sure," the Canadian said, "we'll give it a try."

"Well, that's great," said Elena. "Now I can give you a tour of our city."

Off the freeway, she drove through dark streets past looming warehouses and onto a boulevard with lawn on both sides. To the left rose tall buildings of semi-modern architecture. No comparison to old Quito, this was a city akin to Europe. It was a relief to my eyes that had grown weary of the heavy adobe construction of the colonial Spanish.

Now Elena began speaking again, "This is the main street of Santiago, the Alameda Bernardo O'Higgins, and that over there, on the other side of the plaza, is the Moneda Palace." She was pointing to a low building of solid granite blocks. Dwarfed by its neighbors, grated windows dotted its exterior.

"That is where our President Allende had his offices," she said. "When the military took over, they came in with American planes and bombed it all out. You see how it's shorter than all those around it. Each pilot did such a fine job of diving and strafing just the Moneda that people said they couldn't have been Chilean, they must have been Yankees." She smiled back to where we quietly sat. "But, you know," she continued, "we don't know anything with the military in power."

I made no reply to these comments and shuddered at the possibility of the truth that American pilots had actually carried out attacks during the overthrow of Allende. After several moments of silence, I attempted to change the mood by asking a question. "How come, Elena, there aren't more people on the streets? Certainly the hour isn't terribly late."

"Curfew," she said, waving a finger in the mirror, "curfew, no one is to be out after ten o'clock at night, and it is getting to be that hour now. If you are out the police will pick you up and zip, into prison you go. It has happened to a lot of my friends. Ooooh," her whole body shook, "it's not very good."[5]

We drove on in silence, past the empty downtown and closed shops. Beyond an elegant shopping district, buildings were replaced by individual homes. Stop lights blinked every half mile.

"If you want to take the bus into town tomorrow," Elena once again was speaking, "you must remember where we are going. Buses pass up and down this avenue. When you return, you must remember to get off at this next light."

"You mean where that supermarket is?" I asked.

"Right, I'll give you my mother's address in case you get lost, and her phone number. And be sure to carry your passports."

Turning to the right, we wound through a residential neighborhood, homes spaciously separated, lawns well tended. Several blocks further on, we entered a narrow drive ending at Ana Mendoza's front door. Two stories high, her house was surrounded by shrubbery and a pleasant private yard, certainly not a typical Chilean home.

Ana Mendoza, a gracious hostess, showed us to private rooms, and a bathroom where we could wash. "I'm glad," she said to me before retiring to her own room, "that you speak Spanish. I am very sorry I don't speak your language."

"It's quite all right," I assured her. "Your daughter speaks good English. That's very surprising."

"Oh, she has been to your country many times. I have a son living there now, working for the World Bank. I'll give you his address."

"That would be good," I said. "You have been very kind to invite us here to your home."

---

[5] At least one out of every hundred Chileans was detained for questioning after the coup. At least two thousand of those disappeared and are presumed dead.

"You're welcome. I'm glad to have you, but now we must sleep," and giving me a kiss on the cheek said, "I'll see you in the morning."

Rumbling and rolling as night turned to day led me to believe the country was again exploding, but it was nothing more than an earthquake in the Andes. It got us up and moving, though, for a day of touring and I walked with the Canadians through the central part of town. We inspected the Moneda Palace that Elena had shown us the night before. We looked at the bullet holes and saw where workers were plastering them over, trying to negate the tragedy of the past. We climbed hilltops, through gardens and parks, and were exhausted by the end of the day.

At the supermarket, we bought some delicious Chilean wine, at an incredibly low price. We carried it home intending to share it with Ana and her friends.

Our hostess was home upon our arrival and prepared us a drink before we could uncork the wine. *Pisco* sours for all, a delicious refreshment, far smoother than the jungle *trago* that comes from the same sugar cane. We retired to the back yard as Elena arrived and sat down to chat about the day. The Canadians, speaking English, talked with Elena, and I, speaking Spanish, conversed with her mother.

"Does it bother you Ana," I asked, "to speak about Allende and his Popular Unity Government?"

"Oh, Allende," she looked at me quizzically, and then turned to stare up at the swaying trees. "No, we talk about Allende," and with a nod towards a neighboring yard made an indication that we talk at low levels.

"What did you think of them and the things that they did?," I asked.

"They tried to do good things but it was bad, what happened at the end."

"What do you mean?"

Leaning toward me she said, "They tried to get money to those who work and need it. Some people didn't like it though, and reacted with violence and force. Allende tried to do good but they were programs that just wouldn't work."

"To me," I said, "they seemed like good things that Allende was doing. But I guess he upset the old wealthy class who had lost their position of power. Are those the people that reacted so violently?"

Well, the *Unidad Popular* implemented programs that just wouldn't work. We couldn't get bread and there were all types of shortages."

"So why do you think that was?" I asked.

"I really don't know. There were strange happenings; truck owner strikes and shortages of wheat."

"That may be but I understand that my government along with the Kennecott and Anaconda Copper companies had a lot to do with that."

"I don't think you can blame it on the Americans. Your people have been very kind to me and my family."

"No, it's true," I insisted, "I even read where a striking truck owner said they were receiving CIA money."

"Oh, I really don't know," said Ana. "It was all such a mess."

"Well, I read somewhere that Chile has always exported copper and imported food. When Allende nationalized the copper mines Kennecott and Anaconda convinced my government to cut off all aid and credit[6] and convinced European buyers not to pay for their Chilean copper orders. They figured they would just starve out your country until you rejoined their system."

"Whatever the reason, things were not working well."

"Was most of the country unhappy with Allende," I continued my query, "or did they support what he was doing?"

"There were a lot of people who were behind him and supportive. Despite all the chaos, his popularity was growing."[7]

"So, what ever happened? How did it ever get to the point that the people let the military take over? Certainly that was not normal for Chilean politics."

"People, my friends, were scared. Things were happening that had never happened before."

"So, with encouragement and aid from my country, the military decided it was their duty and right to take over the country?"

"Oh, it was horrible. It was so violent," she shook as she spoke. "They

---

[6] Before Allende was elected Chile received 60 million dollars a year from the US in aid and 200 to 300 million dollars a year in short-term loans from US Banks. Due to pressures from Uncle Sam, multi-lateral loans were essentially cut off and bank credits fell to 30 million dollars a year.

[7] The Popular Unity government received a majority of votes in the 1971 municipal elections and increased their congressional seats in mid-term election in March 1973 — a rare achievement in Chilean Politics.

killed so many people, there was blood in the streets of our beloved Santiago. They were shooting students and people, friends of ours, neighbors." Her bronzed face turned pale as she recalled the scene. Her head drooped lower. "They murdered people in cold blood for no reason at all, put them in prison and tortured them to death. There was no reason, no reason, no reason for all that. Young men and women, mere children shot in the streets . . ."

To Porvenir

MY TIME IN CHILE taught me that war, especially civil war, has consequences. After several days it struck me that there was a significant lack of males in Chile. Whether they had been killed, disappeared, imprisoned, exiled or had fled the country, they were gone. The males who were around all seemed to be in the security forces watching for signs of insurrection. I almost had a run-in with these fellows one evening as they followed me through the Mendoza's neighborhood minutes before the ten o'clock curfew. The prospect of being arrested shivered my soul.

Lack of males led to a longing in the women that was soon out in the open. The night before I left Santiago, Elena's mother, Ana, Mendoza invited me to share her bed with her. The next day, travelling south on a bus through lush vineyards, I fell madly in love with a young, beautiful and warm Chilean woman who was traveling to her home in Villarrica, high in the Chilean Lake District. Slowed by police scouring the bus for unexplained suspects, our journey lasted a pleasantly long time.

Unfortunately, her family whisked her away to her home in the lake counrty and I was left alone in the town of Temuco, an agricultural center of three-story, flat cubicle structures. Here the Mapuches, the indigenous people of Chile who held the whites at bay until 1877, market their wares. I spent hours inspecting fine woolen blankets and the town environs. Agricultural workers occupied drab slat homes on the outskirts of Temuco. During Allende's years they had worked their own land but now they again labored for the *haciendas*. Their homes were set among weeds and hanging laundry surrounded by pigs and chickens groveling in the mud.

After a few days I headed to the mountains and Villarrica, hometown of my new-found love. My approach to the town was signalled by white spires peeking over green poplars. Yellowing fields and groves of autumn trees rose to the right. To the west Lake Villarrica shimmered across forty miles to the misty base of the Andes and Villarrica volcano, crowned on this day by smooth layers of clouds turned a pink hue by the setting sun.

But my beautiful belle had returned to Santiago and I decided to continue south on a circuitous journey through the southern tip of South America and then back up to the States. I began the next leg of my journey behind old Number 557, a classic black steam engine, that puffed out of the roundhouse at daybreak to carry me off. A mighty iron beast, the likes of which are found only on isolated branch lines, it belched smoke high above a single beacon where wind blew it aft over the boiler and cab, the coal car and the wooden-benched passenger coaches.

I was headed for Puerto Montt as far south as land transport reached on the Chilean side of the mountains and as distant from the equator as Boston. In Puerto Montt the traveler can choose either to head east over peaks and lakes to the Argentine town of Bariloche or book passage on a freighter headed a thousand miles south to the Straits of Magellan and Tierra del Fuego. Pondering my options in Puerto Montt's main plaza, I asked a group of giggling high-school girls what I should do. They persuaded me to go south to Punta Arenas and Tierra del Fuego.

Basically a dry-land boy, I had doubts about our rusty-hulled vessel whose main purpose was not catering to passengers but supplying the isolated villages down the coast. In this imposing geography of deserted islands, glaciers, mountains and evergreen forests, I quickly concluded that, should I ever wish, here I could easily divorce myself from my species and the proceedings of its world. In these vast forests, it seemed to me, one could carry on as had the indigenous people of my native northwest hundreds of years ago.

Abandoning such dreams of solo survival, I hooked up with a group of European travelers who were also aboard this old hulk. After four days we were deposited in Punta Arenas, on the Straits of Magellan, where all ships rounding the horn of South America make port. I joined a couple of traveling Brits and together we searched on foot for the ferry to carry us across the straits to Tierra del Fuego. Ominously they checked passports before allowing us on board the ferry.

I was traveling with Harry Diller, a fully bearded, stout fellow who kept us laughing with an ample supply of barroom jokes, and Katherine Crammly, a Welsh tour guide who was doing a little touring of her own. A bit tempermental in the company of jokers like us, she maintained a surprising cheerfulness through this dry and desolate land. When the ferry dropped us off in Tierra del Fuego, it was her womanly wiles that got us a ride on a truck to the small town of Porvenir and it was those same charms that brought us into the oven-warmed kitchen of the Somos o No Somos [Are We or Aren't We] bar and inn, where we found a room for the night.

Fifteen degrees from the Antarctic Circle, Porvenir was chilly at this time of year and the wood cook-stove provided the only comfortable spot in this one-story, uninsulated wood building. We joined the establishment's two proprietors in the kitchen, a friendly husband and his somewhat distant wife. An array of characters, whose relationship to the place I never understood, also sat about the kitchen. There were children, fellow workers and friends, and a barmaid, apparently the main attraction of Porvenir; perhaps the only attraction in that sad, dismal town.

As the evening's feast ended, and people left the table, a large fellow, Gustavo Benítez, remained. Our little celebration, occasioned by this man's thirty-eighth birthday, had been a festive affair. Light-complexioned and with a booming voice, he was a bundle of stories, questions and energy. As others drifted away, another Chilean, more retiring, at all times keeping his distance from the table, also stayed. This second fellow was young and frail with deep-set, brooding eyes. He exuded a quixotic aura that left me unsure that his actions would be predictable. Some internal attraction held him to Gustavo, for he grasped with pleasure at every smile and gesture of confidence that Gustavo directed his way.

Katherine, in turn, intrigued Gustavo and it was to her that he directed his conversation. I remained a silent observer, not compelled to join the conversation, yet too interested to depart.

"I'm a prisoner here, you know," he told Katherine.

"A prisoner, how's that?"

"They have me exiled down here, the military government. They call it 'political internment.' I can't leave or communicate with anyone."

"Oh no, why's that?"

"I was a union leader up north."

"Uh huh, what's wrong with that?"

"We were all supporters of the Popular Unity, kept the country running when the factory and truck owners closed down operations. They tried to sabotage the economy but the workers went in and opened up, turned on the lights and machines and re-started prodution. We had to do it if our country was to survive. Those god-damned selfish factory owners would have starved everyone if they could!

"The truck owners, too. We had to take action when nothing was getting transported. That was a good one. Commandeering trucks and running them to the coast and back to get goods. Goons set up roadblocks to stop us and we'd break on through. Sometimes it was close. But the entire country would have withered without it.

"We were organized. For the first time we were really organized and doing it. We were running factories when they had to be run and we were growing and distributing food when it had to be eaten. It was fantastic, incredible, glorious! I loved it!"

I wasn't sure Katherine understood his rapid-fire Spanish but she seemed involved and questioned him further, "So what happened, Gustavo?"

"*El golpe.* [The overthrow.]"

"And?" Katherine prodded.

"Well, they annihilated it, destroyed it all. They outlawed all the organizations and the unions and replaced them with their AIFLD people"[1]

"Who?"

"*Los gringos*, CIA types."

"So what happened to you?" Katherine asked.

Gustavo picked up a bottle of wine, one of several on the table and began filling our three cups. "Here," he said, "a toast to our great organization, a toast to the *comandos comunales y los cordones industriales. Salud!*" Raising his cup in the air, his brawny arm quivering, he brought it down and emptied it in a gulp.

"Gustavo," Katherine asked after swallowing her wine, "so what did you do?"

"Nothing."

"What do you mean, 'nothing'? How did you get here? You must have done something."

"Nope, nothing. When the *golpe* came I said, 'well, that's it. It's over. I have responsibilities. I have a wife and kids. I can't be going out and doing crazy things. I had to take care of my family. When they shot Allende I knew it was over. I stayed home, didn't do a thing."

"So what happened? How come you're here?"

"Later, they came later, six weeks after the coup, in the middle of the night. Tromp-tromp-tromp-tromp-tromp-tromp-tromp-tromp. Banging on my door. They actually broke it in. Of course we were all frightened, my poor children, nobody knew what was going on. 'Señor Benitez,' they said, they screamed, really they screamed as loud as possible, 'come with us!'"

"Is that true?," I broke in. "They really came in the middle of the night?"

"Here, you want more wine?" he asked me. "Have more wine. And you Katherine?" Then after refilling our glasses, he continued, with a distant and sorrowful look, "Is it true they came in the middle of the night? Of course it's true! It was black outside. We were all asleep in our beds when we heard them come."

---

[1] AIFLD, the American Institute for Free Labor Development, is an organization whose President at the time was Peter J. Grace and whose financial support came from the Kennecott Copper Company, IT&T, Chase Manhattan Bank, United Brands (previously United Fruit), Rockefeller Brother's Fund, Pan American World Airlines, First National City Bank, WR Grace and Company and other US multinational corporations. It has a historical connection with CIA activities throughout Latin America.

"Why do they do that?" I asked.

"To scare people, scare our neighbors, scare everybody. That's the way they operate, on a level of terror. There's no humanity in those people — they're beasts."

"So what happened to you?" Katherine pressed on.

"They took me away to prison, first to one and then to another. I had no contact with my family. They didn't even know what had happened to me. I was just gone."

"Have you talked to them yet?"

"After six months they told my wife where I was. I was still in one of their prisons. They had no charges against me and still don't."

"And can you see her now?"

"Oh no, no mail, no communication of any type."

"The prisons," I asked, "what were the prisons like?"

"No, no, no," he said waving his finger back and forth, "of the prisons I can't talk. They are not good to talk about."

My mind wandered and by the time I returned my attention to the surroundings, Katherine and Gustavo were immersed in their discussion. I poured more wine for all and looked around the room.

Sitting eight feet away, on a simple, white, three-legged stool was the young quixotic fellow. He was the only other person in the room. He had said nothing the entire evening. His head affected a slight twitch when he saw me watching him and he averted his eyes. I continued to stare, wondering what his connection was to us, to Porvenir and our birthday host. He stood up and shuffled laterally across the room, eyeing Gustavo, Katherine and then myself. He came to a halt no more than four feet away, his young eyes looking past me, just over my shoulder. After several minutes I stood and stepped toward him, asking in Spanish how he was.

When I addressed him he blinked and his right hand shook.

"How are you?" I asked,.

"Oh, you speak Spanish," he said, a slight smile crossing his face as he relaxed slightly. "But you're an American."

"I am, and yourself, Chilean?"

"Yes."

"From Porvenir?"

"Now I live in Porvenir." He spoke with his head bowed as if inspecting the floor. "I did live in Santiago. I was in the army, a private, when Allende was President."

"You were stationed in Santiago?" I asked in horror.

His face lifted and his eyes quickly shifted away as he said, "I didn't want to kill people. They made me do it," he stammered, his voice growing louder.

"You were there during the *golpe?*"

"Really, I didn't want to kill people. I didn't want to. They made me." His body froze rigid, only his lips moved.

My stomach turned as I asked, "They put you into the street to stop the resistance?"

"It was bloody," his cheeks tightened. "Bodies, people, death everywhere." His eyes seemed to look forward but were actually staring back into his own head. He was describing incredible insanity. His mental images seized his mind and twisted it in so many bizarre directions that he was reduced to a bundle of raw nerves, flashing in a space and consciousness totally outside my own reality or experience.

"I'm sorry," I said and returned to my chair.

Overwhelmed by the tragedy my country had cooperated in creating,[2] I left with my English traveling friends the following day for the far side of the Island and Argentina. As we hiked up deserted streets, wind whipping at our sides, headed for the weekly bus to the frontier, Katherine related one last tale. "Gustavo told me something I don't think you heard last night," she said.

"What was that?"

"He said when the *golpe* happened, the police came and took the brother of the lady who owns the inn. You know her?"

"Sure, the lady who fixed the meals."

"Right. I guess her brother was some kind of a local leader."

"Uh, huh."

"Well, he said they brought him out into the center of the plaza here and executed him before the eyes of the entire town."

---

[2] Besides aiding the destruction of the Allende government, the US government also strongly supported the Chilean military not only before, but also after they came to power. In 1974, immediately after the junta took over, the US sold Chile 75 million dollars in military equipment. In FY 1975 Chileans comprised 60% of the Latin American soldiers trained at the US Army's School of the Americas in Panama.

Argentine Migration

GUN-TOTING MILITARY scrutinized us as we left Porvenir and again when we crossed the Argentine frontier in the plains of Tierra del Fuego. Journeying across vast windswept flatlands, we travelled in a tightly-packed old green bus that once a week made this trip to the Atlantic side of the Island and the barren, Argentine town of Río Grande.

We found quarters in a sparse dormitory which provided a welcome relief from howling Patagonian winds. Stretched on the lower bunk of my assigned, cement cubicle lay a dark-complexioned, slender man.

"You're an American?," he asked after greeting me.

"That's right," I answered, "and you're Argentine?"

"No, Chilean"

"Ho, I just came from your country," I told him. "What brings you here?"

"Work, there is no work in my country these days. But here in Argentina there is lots of work. So here I am earning money. I couldn't do that in Chile."

"Why is it you can't find work in Chile?" I asked as I stuffed my pack under his bunk and swung to the upper bed for a few minutes of rest.

"Oh, the military. They're a bunch of dunderheads. They don't know how to run an economy," he said.

"That's too bad," I sighed. "Things aren't so good?"

Oh, nobody can get jobs; it's terrible. But Argentina is good, lots of work, especially down here. If you're staying long, I can get you a job."

"No thanks, I'm just passing through. I'm off to Ushuaia tomorrow," I told him.

"Ushuaia," he mused, "it's a beautiful place. I hear there's lots of work there too. Stop on your way back through and tell me how it is."

Twenty-four hours later we were there. Ushuaia, the southernmost town in the world, protected by the tip of the Andes, sits on the shores of Beagle Channel, named after Darwin's ship, The Beagle. A poor, picturesque fishing village, it had recently been discovered by adventure seekers and tour operators catering to the idle-rich. A grand luxury hotel rose on its waterfront. Jets landed at its airport.

Katherine, Harry and I stayed several days, sleeping in a hostel and climbing the glaciers during the day. An old Peace Corps friend, Cristóbal Sczescy, having tracked me all the way from Punta Arenas, ran into us on the main street.

We all left together in an old twin-engine, high-wing, converted Argentine military craft that lifted us above the mountains, over the desolate northern end of Tierra del Fuego, and into the windswept reaches of Patagonia on the Argentine mainland. We flew first to Calafate, sixty miles from Ventisquero Moreno, a live glacier calving and crashing ninety feet into majestically blue Lago Argentina. Calafate, surrounded by blowing sands, was another dreary town in a series of dreary towns in a drab and dreary desert. From there we flew to Comodoro Rivadavia on the Atlantic coast and for a diversion, I waited an entire day attempting to hitchhike up the winding, lonely road towards Buenos Aires. As night fell and I pondered my isolation in the barrens of Patagonia, a coal truck lumbered to a halt. Two burly Argentine truckers motioned for me to throw my pack on top of the coal and to climb into the cab.

They were headed to Bahía Blanca six hundred miles north, on a twenty-four-hour-a-day non-stop haul with one man sleeping while the other one drove. My assigned task was to keep the driver awake with idle chat. After a solid night and day through colorless terrain, my talk became muddled and my mind addled. I opted out of another seventy-two hours of this routine at a gas pump outside San Antonio Oeste, a coastal town on the southern reaches of the rail line that connects Buenos Aires and the Andean town of Bariloche.

Semana Santa, Holy Week, is a time of vacations and celebrations throughout Latin America. In San Antonio Oeste, there was no celebration. Dust blew in the shack-lined streets; only the sea promised diversion. I stagnated in a stagnant town till an urge moved me to the train station for a seventeen-hour ride to Buenos Aires.

Heading north toward the *pampas*, the train entered heavy cultivation as the day turned to night. I slept till the sun rose on the farthest outskirts of the Argentine capital. The train sped into Buenos Aires as trains speed into cities around the world, along tracks beside more tracks strewn with debris and shacks from years gone by. Traveling through the world's southern extremities I had not seen a city of any size in quite a while. I was now startled by the vast subterranean subway network that pulses beneath this metropolis. It transported me through miles of a sunless labyrinth. Disoriented, I stepped off the subway car onto a cold, tile platform and mounted a staircase into glorious sunlight filtering through leafy trees which hung over broad lawns where elderly gentlemen sat feeding pigeons from wrought iron park benches. What I thought would be a congested traffic circle proved instead to be a sedate and pleasant park on a Saturday morning. On the far sideside I could see a curving street with occasional traffic and beyond it rows of well kept buildings.

Off I strolled, lugging my worldly possessions on my back to find a place to sleep. I had arrived at Calle Florida, an elegant pedestrian thoroughfare of fancy shops. I inquired about a room at several walk-up *residencias* but they were filled with Semana Santa vacationers.

Elegance ended at the Avenida de Mayo. Tired and exasperated, I continued my search down two rather depressing blocks. A sign indicated a hotel on the third floor of a large stone building and I gave it a try. An old iron lift elevated me three floors to a bank of frosted windows which had "Hotel de Mayo" printed across the middle. Locked double doors blocked my entrance.

Tapping at the window, pushing the bell, I received no response and was left standing in despair. Tap, tap, ring, ring, tap, tap, ring, ring, ring. Nothing, no one came. The door wouldn't open. Trapped in a tiny lobby, homeless in a great metropolis. Tap, tap, tap. Silence. Then tk, tk, tk, tk, tk, tk, tk, klshlk. The knob turned, the door opened, a short ,pleasant, rotund man allowed me to enter.

Once inside I greeted him and, having despaired in my search for a private room, I simply asked, "Do you have a bed I can rent?"

"A bed? That's all you want?," he smiled as he answered. "That I do have. Here, let me show you."

I followed him around the corner through a marvelously tiled foyer that reached up past stories of encircling rooms to an open skylight and the clouds above. He led me down a narrow corridor and stopped before a dimly lit doorway. After fiddling with a handful of keys he opened the door to reveal dank, narrow quarters with one window high on the far wall, two beds and two large clothes bureaus.

"It will cost you seven *pesos* (fifty cents) a night," he told me. "The bed behind the door is yours. Your roommate will be back soon. He's Uruguayan. I'm sure he'll be all right."

My roommate was there when I woke from a short nap. Seated on his bed, he sipped from a decorated wooden straw plunged deep into a gourd of green *yerba-mate* mush, the local tea. A tall angular fellow, he produced an easy youthful smile as I opened my eyes. Indirect light came through the one window. The bare bulb on the ceiling hadn't been lit.

"*Buenas tardes*, my friend," he saluted me once my eyes had opened.

"*Buenas tardes*," I returned, "I hope you don't mind my intrusion into your room."

"Not at all, you're quite welcome. There's easily room enough for us both."

"My name is Jim Tarbell," I rose to shake his hand.

"And mine is Federico Santoyo. I am pleased to meet you."

"Our landlord tells me that you're Uruguayan."

"Quite right. I hail from across the mouth of the great Rio de la Plata. Here in Buenos Aires to make myself some money."

"So, what's your line of work? How long are you here for?"

"Well, the government of Argentina doesn't know I'm here, so I can't say how long I'll stay. But right now I'm working on some roofing jobs. I earn plenty of money."

"How come you're not in Uruguay?"

"Oh, things are terrible there, especially since the military took over. There are no jobs and they're constantly throwing people in jail. It's a real mess, very sad."[1]

"Huh," I mused, "I was thinking of visiting your country on my way back to the States. You think that's a good idea?"

"Visit Uruguay? No, no need. It used to be a beautiful spot, but now it's run down and dirty. No one is happy. I wouldn't go there. It's much better here in Buenos Aires. This is the last refuge from repression."[2]

"Well, I'll have to reflect on that," I told him, "Meanwhile, I'm off to find something to eat."

Walking the street, I found a good restaurant. Over the next week I found many of them; Big plates of spaghetti with salad for fifty cents and free table wine served in place of water! Life was so inexpensive, I couldn't afford to leave and I spent days eating fine meals and strolling Buenos Aires' broad boulevards.

The avenues of Buenos Aires are often divided by grassy strips and crossing them required several stages. One day as I crossed the Avenida 9 de Julio, one of the widest thoroughfares in the world, a short swarthy man wearing well-worn deep blue trousers and a bulky sweater approached. He appeared more like an Ecuadorian construction worker than a Buenos Aires resident.

---

[1] Uruguay, traditionally the model (along with Chile) of South American democracy, had always been an enlightened leader in social reforms. In 1973 this changed with the introduction of military rule and soon Uruguay had more political prisoners per capita than any other country in the world.

[2] A year later, the Argentine military took over, instituting yet another right-wing military regime that proved more horrifying than any of the other military regimes in Latin America. With this change almost all of South America was under military rule installed largely because democracy was leading these countries away from the dictates of the industrialized capitalist world. In each case these military governments were heavily supported by US military and economic assistance.

"Excuse me, *Señor*," he said as we passed on one of the grassy median strips. "Can you help me?"

"Perhaps," I responded curiously, "what do you need?"

"I need work," he told me. "Do you know any place where I can find some work?"

"Oh, I'm just a visitor from the United States," I said, "I don't know anything about Buenos Aires. Have you looked hard?"

"I've been looking very hard for several days, but I can't find anything."

"Are you from Buenos Aires?"

"No," he said, lowering his eyes, "I'm from Chile, Santiago."

"Is that right?" I said with sudden understanding. "Here, why don't we sit down on this bench?"

We sat on a bench in the middle of this grass strip in the middle of perhaps the broadest and busiest intersection in the world, traffic whizzing by on all sides. Three blocks in front of us a three-hundred-foot obelisk rose in commemoration of the 400th anniversary of the founding of Buenos Aires. In this setting of speed, extravagance and grandeur, this man told me his tales of woe.

"Why did you come here to Buenos Aires?" I asked.

"I had to," he replied. "My wife and children are starving; there is no work in Chile."

"I'm sorry. Things aren't good there, huh?"

"They're horrible," he lamented.

"Is it worse than it was during Allende's time?" I asked.

"Oh, much worse. Then a man could get a job and some food. Now he can get nothing. Things are terrible."

"I'm sorry," I said. "My country is giving lots of support to the military there and backing the present economic regimen.[3] Apparently it's not doing the Chilean people much good, but, you know, I might be able to help you."

"How is that?," he asked, his expression brightening quickly.

---

[3] Once the military took over in Chile, the US resumed aid and became the junta's backbone of support. Besides military aid, in 1975 the US provided 91 million dollars in direct aid to Chile, rescheduled a 95 million dollar Chilean debt and prevailed upon multilateral institutions to supply another 90 million dollars in credit. Without this aid, the military junta in Chile would not have survived.

"I'm sharing a room with an Uruguayan who is here working. He might be able to tell me where you can get a job."

"Oh, that would be very good, any kind of a job," he assured me. "I have no more money and my family is hungry. I travelled all the way here and now I can't find work. It would be very good if you could ask him."

"I'll definitely talk to him," I told him, "but then how can I get hold of you?"

"I'm staying in a room. I can give you the address. You could get hold of me there," he said.

"Good, write it down on this piece of paper and I'll go see him right now. Will you be there in a few hours?"

"If I'm not, you can leave a note. I'm going to keep looking for a job."

"All right," I said, "good to talk to you. I'll see you later. *Ciao*."

"Thank you for your help," he said shaking my hand. "*Ciao!*"

I returned to my room where I found Federico sitting in the dark on his bed, complacently sipping *yerba mate*.

"Good Afternoon, Federico," I greeted him, "I have a request for you."

"*Sí*, Jim, what can I do for you?"

I described my conversation with the Chilean and his need for a job. With an understanding eye, Federico happily supplied information on the illicit underworld of undocumented immigrant employment. He carefully transcribed the directions onto a note. They were a bit complicated; one had to go to an appointed cafe at a certain hour, from where he proceeded with others to another location and so on.

Referring to a large Buenos Aires map, I located the Chilean's address and slipping the vital job data in my pocket, I hurried back onto the streets. The journey required taking several subways to a distant part of town and I once again emerged in the middle of a park. Here the grass was dry, the buildings old and not so tall, the streets not so well kept and the pedestrians not so elegant. The address I was looking for proved to be a bar several blocks from the park.

I entered through swinging frosted-glass doors into a simple establishment of bare wood tables. Behind the bar a large Argentine tender in a white apron washed mugs. Leaning on the plywood countertop, I asked if he knew my Chilean friend.

Giving me a quizzical stare, he eyed me up **and down**. "Who do you want?," he demanded.

"Do you know this Chilean?," I asked showing him the name and address the Chilean had written. "He told me he was staying here. I have a note for him."

"Who is this man?," the bar tender grilled me.

"Do you know him?" I persisted, "I have this note for him."

"A note, what's the note about?"

"Well, if you know him, tell me."

"What's the note about?" he insisted leaning closer towards my face.

"He's looking for a job," I reluctantly told him. "It's information about where he can get a job."

Several heads in the bar swung around with this comment.

The bar tender grumbled, "Yeah, I know him, but he's not here now."

"Well could you take the note and give it to him when he comes back?"

"Yeah, here, give it to me."

"Thanks," I said and slipped out the door.

That was the last I heard of the matter. The Chilean never got in touch with me and Federico didn't know if he had shown up for work. I left Buenos Aires a few days later headed north through Paraguay and Brazil back to the States.

Back to the Bowels of the Beast

SMOG! Low visibility and thick haze over Miami greeted Varig flight 199 from Belem, Brazil, in early May 1975. After two years of clean air, blue skies and white sandy beaches throughout South America, this blur out the window was a shock.

My plan had been to hitchhike from Miami airport to DC, but that idea was aborted by the array of twisting and gliding freeway ramps outside the glass terminal doors. I couldn't hike my way through that maze, so, back in the States, land of instant gratification and wanton consumption, I decided to fly. A few seconds with the computerized ticket machine and I spent more for my two hour flight than most Ecuadorians earn in a year. American Airlines to Washington National — after several years, home again.

What now? Of my old Capitol Hill companions, few remained. Watergate and its attendant Republican debacle had swept away most of my old cronies. I'd once served double martinis to the guy now in the White House, but I doubted he would remember and wrote off any thoughts of snoozing at 1600 Pennsylvania Avenue.

I did know that one fine friend, Mary Beth Heister, the fantasy of my younger years, was still in town and it was to her that I now turned. In those earlier days of swinging in parks and dancing on rooftops, she had worked down the hall for an old Pennsylvania Congressman from the right side of the aisle. Since that time she had moved to the lobbyist's world and was now captivating politicians in the interests of Kennecott Copper, a firm I knew from its notorious Chilean reputation.

So I was off, backpack in tow, across the Potomac in the hazy sunshine to downtown DC. Dizzying traffic cloged the streets and rigid square structures, power centers of the world's most influential corporations, rose skyward. Large block numerals —1919 L Street — marked the entrance of an edifice larger and shinier than its neighbors. As is the custom in these modern keepers of the world's businesses, a solitary guard stationed behind a mahogany desk surveyed the passing crowd. He picked me out instantly as I moved toward the double elevator doors in my long curly locks and tattered green backpack.

"Hey you, where are you going?"

After two-and-a-half years in the land of the *patrón*, where they back up authority with the snout of a large gun, meekness took over in the face of this six-three frame barking orders. I tried to act as if my grubby Levi's and week-old beard fit in with the coat-and-tie freaks pouring through the throbbing elevator doors, but failed miserably. A cold sweat formed on my skin. Back in America, I wasn't part of the club. Something had changed, not only without but also within.

In time, I persuaded the guard to phone the offices of Kennecott Copper. Even after I was cleared by Mary Beth he was doubtful. He let me into the elevators, but not my backpack; that stayed under his care in the lobby.

Up I swooshed, fourteen floors to carpeted halls, beige walls and soft lighting. Muzak receded behind the silently closing elevator doors. Down the corridor I found "Kennecott Copper, Office of Washington Services."

It was behind this door that Kennecott Copper had coordinated activities with the US government after the Popular Unity government nationalized their mines in Chile. Kennecott had cut off all payments to Chile for copper, persuaded the US government to attach Chilean bank accounts, discouraged European countries from buying Chilean copper and put pressure on the Chilean government to change its ways. Uncle Sam reacted with the infamous instructions of Richard Nixon: "Make the Chilean economy scream!" This move by the US government led to the overthrow of Chilean democracy, which I had heard about continuously the past several months. It was behind this door that plans leading to the death of tens of thousands of supporters of the democratic Chilean government had been plotted.

As I took hold of the knob, my body and soul shuddered.

Turning the knob I entered — into the very bowels of the beast.

In a flowing black dress and with familiar blond hair, Mary Beth ran from the rear and gave me a welcome-home hug. Then taking my arm, she escorted me to her inner office.

"So how," she asked, holding my arm tightly and fixing me with her quizzical stare, "was South America?"

Stunned by my sudden presence with an old friend in the belly of a reviled monster, I surveyed the room before responding. "Pretty nutty," I said, "lots of things going on down there. Some good, some not so good. But tell me, how is it working for Kennecott Copper and what do you do for these people here?"

"Mmmmm, it's all right," she replied, gently releasing my arm and indicating a long row of filing boxes. "See all these files? I watch every piece of legislation that goes through Congress. That way Kennecott can act on any bill of the slightest interest to them."

As I sank into a chair, despair over the power of the corporate world engulfed me. "Oh, that's great," I said. "How do you like helping these guys?"

Holding me with her innocent eyes she asked, "What do you mean by that?"

I rallied as I thought of my two-and-a-half years in South America: the faces of the old ladies carrying grain sacks, the tinted glass of the Mercedes, the tranquillity and peace of Lago San Pablo and Pachijal, the anonymity of the corporate offices, the blood in the streets. "It's a long story," I told her, "but it's one you should hear."

Afterword

I SURVIVED my days in military-dominated South America. Not all of us did.

On March 21, 1979, Emil Peterson, storyteller, bon vivant, archeologist, apartment hunter and roommate extraordinaire wrote that he would start taking photos to accompany these stories. On July 27, 1981, the American embassy in Santiago, Chile informed his family that he was dead. The US Embassy and Chilean police claimed Emil had fallen and hit his head on a bedpost. His mother, however wrote that when she finally received his body back in Council Bluffs, Iowa that, "He was bruised and stabbed all over; his skull was broken completely apart, one ear nearly off, one eye pushed back into his skull, knees were broken, etc." No explanation was ever given.

Also Available from Ridge Times Press

RIDGE REVIEW.
A magazine. 1981 - present. $10.00 per year.
Covering the economic, political and social world of the northern
California Coast with in-depth investigative reporting, Ridge Review is a
model for the compilation of information that every community needs to
manage its affairs. Topics covered to date in separate issues: media, agriculture, water, work, housing, justice, retirement, the ocean, money, health
industry, rivers, education, sheep, orchards, crafts, salmon, fishing, inten-
tional communities, timber, marijuana, tourism, politics, land use, the
wine industry, endangered species, music, garbage, and local control.

CASH CROP: An American Dream
by Ray Raphael. 1985. $8.00
The inside story of the marijuana boom in the California backcountry, as
told by the people who grow marijuana and the people who oppose it.
Cash Crop is a true and honest account of how an illegal industry affects
the lives of ordinary people. A unique self-portrait of a community in crisis.

COMMUNITY DESIGN PRIMER
by Randolph T. Hester, Jr.. 1990. $20.00
An indispensable guide for any community set on determining their own
future. Written by internationally recognized University of California
Landscape Architecture Professor Randy Hester this primer is designed for
grass roots organizations that want to gain control over their community
and the way it is designed.

FOLLY AND TANTRUM
by Beca Lafore
1984. Out of print
In and out of freedom and order, madness and reality, Beca Lafore weaves
us through the folly and tantrum of youth born in the harshness of modern
society. Poetry.

Please enclose $2.00 with each order for postage and handling. California
residents add 6% sales tax. Send orders to Ridge Times Press, P. O. Box 90,
Mendocino, California 95460.

This book was typeset in Goudy and Chantilly in Quark Express on a Mac II CI. It was printed on recycled, sixty-pound book paper on a Heidelbreg MO/E offset press at Black Bear Press in Caspar, California.